INTEGRATIVE MANAGEMENT

Developmental Management

General Editor: Ronnie Lessem

Charting the Corporate Mind*
Charles Hampden-Turner

Managing in the Information Society
Yoneji Masuda

Developmental Management
Ronnie Lessem

Foundations of Business
Ivan Alexander

Greening Business
John Davis

Ford on Management*
Henry Ford

Managing Your Self
Jagdish Parikh

Managing the Developing Organization
Bernard Lievegoed

Conceptual Toolmaking
Jerry Rhodes

Transcultural Management
Albert Koopman

Integrative Management
Pauline Graham

Executive Leadership
Elliot Jaques

* For copyright reasons this edition is not available in the USA

Developmental MANAGEMENT

Integrative Management

CREATING UNITY FROM DIVERSITY

PAULINE GRAHAM

WITH A FOREWORD BY
RONNIE LESSEM

Basil Blackwell

Quotations from Mary Parker
Follett's *Dynamic Administration* are by
kind permission of Pitman Publishing

First published 1991

Basil Blackwell Ltd
108 Cowley Road, Oxford, OX4 1JF, UK

Basil Blackwell Inc.
3 Cambridge Center
Cambridge, Massachusetts 02142, USA

British Library Cataloguing in Publication Data

A CIP catalogue record for this book is available from the British Library.

Library of Congress Cataloging in Publication Data
Graham, Pauline.
Integrative management: creating unity from diversity / Pauline
Graham; with a foreword by Ronnie Lessem.
p.   cm.—(Developmental management)
Includes bibliographical references and index.
ISBN 0-631-17391-9
1. Management.   2. Executive ability.   3. Psychology, Industrial.
I. Title.   II. Series.
HD38.G68   1991
658.4'09—dc20
90-43143
CIP

Typeset in 11 on 13pt Ehrhardt
by Hope Services (Abingdon) Ltd.
Printed in Great Britain by
T. J. Press Ltd.,
Padstow, Cornwall

TO ZOE
My beloved granddaughter

Contents

Foreword: Integrative Management

by Ronnie Lessem

Introduction

Half Way to the Euro-company

The business magazine *International Management*[1] in May of 1990, brought to our attention the European Economic Interest Grouping (EEIG): 'Whereas more conventional cross-border structures such as subsidiaries and joint ventures consume mountains of paper, time and expensive legal advice, the EEIG is a breeze by comparison.' All you have to do is find a willing partner in at least one other EC country and register your new entity's name with your local registrar of commerce. Claiming that the EEIG was taking us 'halfway to the Euro Company', the article went on to explain that the new mechanism left great scope for cross-border linkages in the form of:

- shared research and development;
- jointly commercialized licences for new technologies;
- pooled purchasing and distribution arrangements;
- coordinated production, transport and delivery schedules;
- joint bids on public works and supply contracts;
- joint marketing and sales activities; and
- joint venture contracts with companies outside the Community.

So much for the legal mechanism. But what sort of business and social enterprise would lend itself towards such cooperative, cross-border and cross-company activities?

The Role of Mary Parker Follett

Strangely enough, the theory underlying such joint ventures, whether within or without the organization, was developed not in the 1980s, as such ventures began to proliferate, but in the 1920s, when they had scarcely been dreamed of.

The far-sighted individual concerned was an American political scientist and social activist, Mary Parker Follett, who also exerted a strong influence on the more enlightened members of the British business community of her time. The Cadburys and the Rowntrees are particular cases in point. Remarkably, Follett's work has been almost completely ignored in Europe and America (the Japanese have taken her thinking much more closely to heart!), until now, when it has been resurrected, aptly enough, by another woman, similarly cosmopolitan in her culture and activities.

Follett graduated from high school at the tender age of 12, and went on to study at Harvard, in America, and then at Cambridge, in England. Her first book on the American political system attracted the attention of Theodore Roosevelt, who declared it essential reading for any study of Congressional government. However, Follett was not content to remain an academician and, very quickly, she proved herself to be a social innovator, turning lacklustre schools into vibrant community centres. The self-governing centres she established in Boston became models for the rest of the country.

In fostering self-government she combined her roles, then, as both scholar and as manager. Moreover, she saw the creativity of the group process as the critical enabling feature of self-government. In effect, some seventy-five years ago, she was advocating the replacement of bureaucratic institutions by group networks. As she became heavily involved, herself, in public tribunals and industrial relations her attention shifted from public to private enterprise. When the first Department of Business Administration was opened at the London School of Economics in 1933 Follett was asked to give the inaugural lectures. She adopted the theme of 'Freedom and Coordination', maintaining that the business world 'is never again to be directed by individual intelligences, but by intelligences interacting and ceaselessly influencing one another. There is, of course, competition between our large firms, but the cooperation between them is coming to occupy a larger and larger relative place.'[2] Follett saw the light some sixty years before it really began to shine.

From Egypt to Britain

In the mid 1960s, when all but the Japanese were looking the other way, a woman, of Spanish extraction, born and French-educated in

Egypt and settled in England, rediscovered Follett. Pauline Graham, trained as an accountant and ran her accountancy practice of consortia companies dealing with capital projects in Eastern Europe and Latin America. Then, she changed course and went into general management in the retail trade. Here, having to lead large numbers of people, she came across the daily realities of managing. Perhaps because she is a woman, perhaps because she is a mother, she could not wholeheartedly accept the then prevailing received wisdom and attitudes on how best to manage. She preferred to follow the dictates of her own common sense. She also wanted to know why she was at variance with the others, why she rejected their complacency and their apparently divine right to manage, by the mere fact of their appointment. So, she read and she studied and, almost inevitably, was led towards Mary Parker Follett. Graham's book, *Integrative Management*, written twenty-five years later, is both an upgrading and an application of Follett's management philosophy. It also paves the way – much more than half the way – towards the new Euro-company.

Integrative Management

Business and Society

The Concept of Partnership

After that long stint in financial management of huge capital projects Pauline Graham, deciding to change course, went into the very different field of retail management and joined the John Lewis Partnership. The company today has over 16,000 partner–employees and is recognized worldwide as a model of industrial democracy. What is less well known, though, is the functioning of the Partnership 'registrar'. Such a registrar must always be a woman and every trading branch of this retailing group must have one. Although possessing no executive responsibilities the registrar stands, in terms of status and authority, equal to the general manager.

Quite simply, as Graham illustrates, the founder of the Partnership, John Spedan Lewis, equated the management of the business with that of the family. Just as in the traditional family the husband was the go-getter and aggressive breadwinner and the wife the peacemaker and the upholder of the family's conscience, so, Spedan Lewis concluded, it had to be in the business. The general manager was there to make the profits but the registrar, a woman by his side, had to ensure that these were achieved fairly and justly. To enable her to do this the manager had to keep her continuously informed of what was happening on the business side of the operation, and she had to keep him in touch with the spirit, tone and morale of the branch.

Interestingly enough, whereas the Japanese have very successfully internalized their family structure into the business community, we in Europe and America have not succeeded in doing the same. The John Lewis Partnership, therefore, is an enlightening exception to the norm, truly combining masculine and feminine principles of business competition and social cooperation.

Updating the Business Ethic

A business, Graham argues, cannot be abstracted exclusively into an economic entity. The best of our corporations, like the John Lewis Partnership, are very directly engaged in creating a better-ordered and a more just society. As business enterprise becomes the dominant force on the global stage so its roles and responsibilities are enriched and enhanced. 'Only a root and branch review of the business ethic which recognizes private enterprise as one of the building blocks of democratic society', according to Graham, will do.

Whereas neither Parker Follett nor Pauline Graham are the first business philosophers to address the issue of business's role in society, they have been the first to place the principles of relatedness, connectedness, and joint endeavour so firmly in the political and economic foreground.

The Group Factor

The Individual and the Group

The primary unit of economics or of society, Follett insisted, is not the individual enterprise or the person in isolation. The assumption that a man or woman, a school or business, thinks and feels independently of outside influences is arid intellectualism that does not accord with the facts. There is no such thing as a separate ego with a separate existence of its own. The unit of society is the group–individual.

In one sense, then, Follett is in tune with the group-orientated

Japanese. In another sense, though, she retains her identification with a Western style of individuality. For she argues that the more diverse the groups that the individual belongs to, the more he or she develops as a person. Interestingly enough, the more diverse the associations in which the enterprise is engaged, the more it develops as a business and cultural entity.

Inter-group Relations

The relations of individuals within groups, of groups within an organization, and of groups of organizations amongst one another, are based on both competition and cooperation. Both are necessary to evolution and progress. However, in today's economic arena there is an undue imbalance between the two. Hence Europe is only half way towards a state of integration.

In fact the effects of cooperation are, on the whole according to Graham, superior to those of competition. The individual, in him or herself, is a composite being, woven of many parts. Managers do not do their job well unless they help the individuals in their group to develop their integrity, connect their group with others in the company and connect their firm with people and groups in other companies. The model of an interdependent commercial ecosystem is becoming ever more appropriate than that of an economy of independent enterprises. Such an ecosystem is made up of living organisms rather than dead mechanisms.

Relating, Coordinating, Controlling

The Organic Management Process

At the heart of an organic as opposed to a mechanistic management process, then, lies the activity of 'relating' as opposed to controlling. Recognition of this has been obscured by the military and ecclesiastical heritage with which management has been 'scientifically' imbued. Not surprisingly, Mary Parker Follett and Pauline Graham, nurturers as well as hunters, have redressed this imbalance.

Follett recognized the managing process as the organizing activity that goes on in the plant, the animal, individual or group. Her vantage point was social and biological rather than political and institutional. The process as she saw it 'related', 'coordinated' and 'controlled' various sub-systems, integrating them into a functioning and functional unit.

Managing Effectively

Managing effectively, as a result, involves not aggregation but integration. The manager, with his work-group or joint venture, creates a whole out of the factors at his disposal. The essential nature of unity, Graham argues, is order. Order between sub-parts is one of relation, not of addition. For that reason, effective action results from direct communication between all those who can influence the situation, and the earlier such interaction begins the better.

Perhaps the best known illustration of such effective coordination is the Japanese *kan-ban* (just-in-time) method of production, where the manufacturer is in close relations with his sub-contractors. Due to the continuous and reciprocal exchange of information, neither he nor they need to build large stocks in anticipation of production. Moreover, for the exchange of information to be fully reciprocal mutual trust is of the essence. Trust cannot be imposed. It has to be learnt through practice and earned. Yet trust should not preclude healthy conflict.

Integrating Differences

Follett and Graham, as democratic Westerners, prefer conflict to conformity. Diversity, for them, is the most essential feature of life, as it is for the European Community, and fear of difference is dread of life itself. Treated as such an expression of legitimate difference, conflict can be used as the spur to find the wider solution, that which will meet the mutual interests of the different parties involved.

There are, then, three ways of dealing with conflict. Domination or compromise, the first two of these, merely serve to settle conflicts, and not to resolve them. The third way, that of integration, is based on the idea of joining powers instead of setting them against each other. It occurs, according to Follett, when a solution is found that allows both parties to find their place in it and when neither sacrifices anything of significance to them. For that to happen there needs to be joining of powers.

Growing Joint Power

Power-Over Versus Power-With

Follett had studied the subject of power in political science, and in philosophy, and was able to bring her wider outlook into management. She was therefore one of the first people to import the study of power into the teaching of management.

Almost invariably, when we think of power and how to use it, we think of the power we can exercise over others, or which they can impose on us. The basic premise is of opposing, antagonistic sides. Yet establishing relations – whether political or industrial – on the basis of 'over' and 'under' others does not produce quality work. In comparing the workmanship of, for example, the Japanese or the Germans, in comparison with, for instance, the British or Americans, Follett's thesis is immediately borne out.

So the trend today, amongst the more enlightened British and American managers, is towards some degree of power sharing. Follett thought differently. She came to the conclusion that, in reality, we cannot share or transfer genuine power, that is, the individual's capacity to act. For power resides in experience, in knowledge, and in personal competencies which are specific to the individual. The desirable alternative to managers exercising 'power-over', therefore, is not power sharing. Management should make it its business to give workers the power to grow capacity or power for themselves.

Whereas in power sharing, managers share their power with their workers, all going one way, in 'power-with', the notion is of joining powers, of both managers and workers pooling their respective powers into the common pot, with the current flowing both ways. Such power-with, then, can be extended to relations not only between workers and management but between commerce and industry, business and government, or manufacturer and sub-contractor.

Making Power Grow

Follett's thesis is therefore clear. The more that powers are channelled individually and collectively – in terms of capacity to do – the more genuine power there is. Managers therefore have to get to know the actual and potential powers of the people and institutions with whom they are connected. They should then provide the climate, facilities and learning opportunities through which these can be successfully developed. This involves effective management and empathetic leadership.

Leading and Following

Leadership Versus Management

Pauline Graham decries the currently fashionable split between leading and managing. The history of business, she says, is littered with examples of visionaries who failed because of their ignorance or neglect of routines. The view that crowns the leader as 'supremo', the one that provides the inspiration and charisma, and the managers as the people who merely master the routines is simply, Graham says, divisive and out of date. It is harking back to the old days of the dichotomy between 'thinking' and 'doing'.

The Function of the Leader

Follett summarized the function of the leader/manager as that of 'group accomplishment on a continuing basis'. This comprised:

- defining the common purpose, communally and strategically;
- determining the mode of association both within and without the enterprise;
- building the future – the successful leader sees in his mind's eye the new situation before it becomes actuality;
- sharing experience, thereby creating a milieu that allows for mutuality;
- turning followers into leaders.

Group accomplishment on a continuing basis, in effect, obeys the law of the situation rather than the rules of the organization or the personal dictats of a duly installed leader.

Obeying the Law of the Situation

Letting the Facts Speak for Themselves

When I was first introduced by my academic colleagues to Parker Follett, albeit in much watered down vein, it was to 'the law of the situation' that I was exposed.

In the traditional view of the organization the individual acts as directed from above and in turn imposes his direction on his subordinates. Authority and responsibility are essentially based on order taking and order giving. This is a view that satisfied neither Parker Follett nor Pauline Graham. For Follett, then, one person should not give orders to another, but both should agree to take their orders from the situation.

By developing the concept of 'the law of the situation', Follett at one stroke depersonalized orders. She maintained that when a situation is seen in its entirety it has its own order and logic.

The authority is inherent in the situation. When a manager examines any situation carefully, he will find significant facts which then speak for themselves and determine action.

Real Versus Delegated Authority

It is the task, the activity to be carried out, then, which is the source of real authority. Each situation has its own law. Authority belongs to the job and stays with the job; the power to exercise it attaches to the individual posted for the time being to it. Real authority then resides in the task, and the power attaches to the individual doing it. Like personal power, it cannot be delegated.

This is not a welfarist notion, as Graham puts it, but a plain necessity. The manager today has therefore to establish in his or her section or company a mode of association in which joint activity can take place and collective responsibility take root and grow, making for work of a high and highly satisfying order.

Thus the personal responsibility of everyone in the business, and of those associated with it, is a prerequisite for the success of the enterprise. At least that is the case for what Graham terms 'the new managers', or our societal leaders, who will have been duly influenced by the new physics.

The New Managers

The Integral Person

Advances in physics, Graham emphasizes, have impacted on psychology and, thereby, on our perceptions of the nature of people. The machine-like view of nature has been abandoned, at least in part, in favour of a holographic concept which is based on the complex interconnections between sub-systems and systems. As a result the idea that personality is exclusively made up of a controlling trait should give way to the view that human beings have diverse traits in themselves, as well as between themselves. As a result, greed and selfishness, like competitiveness, whilst forming part of human nature, can be, and are, integrated with generosity and cooperation to form a more harmonious whole.

In the same way as individuals, then, are multifaceted so are organizations. Therefore cooperation between the different facets is required if either person or group is to function effectively. Each work group, moreover, is a nuclear community in its own right; as a work group, it connects with other groups within its internal community. But the organization is not only this limited community; it also consists of its suppliers, its customers, and all the other individuals and institutions with which it has ties. The business or business association, as a whole, therefore becomes a networked combination of multifaceted groups, which I have termed a 'molecular organization'.[3]

Business in Society

Follett argued, given the many-faceted nature and the interconnectedness of individual and enterprise, that the role of business was to engage in reciprocal service:

A group of people settling in a new region first plant and sow. But other things have to be done. One buys groceries and sells to one's neighbours. One does this expecting someone else in the community to build one's store and house and keep them in repair, and someone else to make one's shoes . . . This is an exchange, or interchange of services. When we say *reciprocal service* it seems to me that we are nearer the facts, and also that we are expressing the give and take of life which is its noblest aspect. That person [or manager] is intellectually or morally defective who is not taking part in this give and take of life.[4]

As we can see, then, whereas Adam Smith focused on the social division of labour, from a self-interested perspective, Mary Parker Follett viewed the same economic and social phenomenon from a reciprocal standpoint.

By focusing on the process of relating, Follett, according to Pauline Graham, grasped the organizing principle itself in a very particular way. She saw its function primarily to be that of coordinating the energies of people, enabling them to work more cooperatively together, thereby evolving both in their personal development and also in their solidarity with one another. The particular organizing process which unites them in cooperative effort in their daily lives makes them better individuals and, as such, makes for social progress. In the work-place the production of tangible goods and of intangible values can combine to make the evolving community who, through tension and conflict but always with that underlying sense of consensus over the give and take of life, can move forward.

The work-place thus becomes an exemplar, as Graham describes it, of the more just society, where 'the new manager', and the members of his or her team, create new values and standards; and these new values and standards are radiated outwards, through the activities of the individual workers in the other groups to which they belong. Thus the better citizen at work becomes the better citizen in society. Our work, Follett said, is to be our highest contribution to our society. What we need to evolve, therefore, is a 'relational' and not a directional view of management. Traditional management and organization theory has always stressed that power, authority, influence and leadership can only be understood within the superior/ subordinate framework. Follett came to different conclusions. Coordination and integration of information and action – as she was advocating seventy years ago and is now being made easier as technology 'informates' – will need to take over from order giving. This applies, quintessentially, to cross-border alliances.

The Whole Way to the Euro-company

Such a relational approach to management, then, will inevitably be required for the successful orchestration of the new joint ventures, and cross-border alliances, emerging in the new Europe. In fact, if full economic and social integration is to be achieved, at both macro and micro levels, the principles and practices of reciprocal service will need to be embedded into management and organization, from the grassroots upwards:

These principles – of *uberrimae fidei*, of fullest disclosure of information, of trust, of being bound by each other's actions, of sharing in the profits and losses of the business, of pooling individual powers – regulate the relations of partners who see themselves as equals between themselves, not as absolutely or uniformly equal, but as each having something unique and different and worthwhile to contribute to the common endeavour, and derive their rights and responsibilities therefrom: an egalitarianism that integrates the different skills and different specialisms but is founded on a commonality of interests and values.[5]

What Follett, and now Pauline Graham, have in fact done is to provide the individual-centred Western hemisphere – notably America and Europe, with the genuine counterpart to the collectively attuned Eastern hemisphere – notably Japan. We shall only succeed in managing joint ventures, in the West, if we reconstruct our relationships within and between individual and organization (part and whole) using the sorts of relational guidelines provided by Follett and Graham. Should we choose to follow them we shall also become developmental managers.

Ronnie Lessem 1991

Notes

1 *International Management*, 'Strained Alliances: The Birth Pangs of Corporate Europe', May 1990.
2 Mary Parker Follett, *The New State*, Longmans, Green, London, 1920, p. 112.
3 Lessem, R., *Developmental Management*, Basil Blackwell, Oxford, 1990.
4 Mary Parker Follett, *Dynamic Administration: the Collected Papers of Mary Parker Follett*, Elliott M. Fox and L. Urwick, eds, Pitman Publishing, London, 1973, p. 104.
5 Pauline Graham, *Integrative Management*, Basil Blackwell, Oxford, 1991.

Introduction

This book is addressed to the practising and aspiring managers who would like to understand better the process and the function of managing so as to become more effective leaders. We live in exciting times, as we move towards our third millennium, with its wide array of creative possibilities at one end, and destructive threats at the other. The rules of the game are changing and no one group of individuals is better placed than the managers, the doers at the sharp end, at altering them for the better.

The winds of change are blowing, bringing new perceptions and ideas which have to battle against entrenched assumptions and received wisdom to achieve acceptance.

In the political field, there have been momentous changes in the countries in Eastern Europe, where people power and grassroots demands for democracy and economic reform have toppled governments. Economic reform is, however, harder to implement than political liberalization. It is not easy to change from a centralized economic system to a market economy. Apart from outside governmental help, the Eastern European countries, as indeed the Soviet Union, also need all the goodwill and know-how of the business managers in the European Community to help them restructure their economies. Whatever arrangements the governments put in place to facilitate exchanges, substantial responsibility lies with the business community to ensure that the hopes aroused by political democratization are translated into a better standard of living for the peoples. A large task, indeed. The advent of the single European market in 1992, not so long ago seen as the high point of Europe's evolution, is now but a stepping-stone to yet greater freedom in trade and wider cooperation within the whole of Europe.

The winds of change are indeed blowing, and not only in the

political sphere. In the business and managerial fields, too, there are fundamental shifts in our views about organizations and of the place of business in society. Most of us are aware, on the whole, of these changes. Awareness, however, is not enough. The requirement is that we develop this awareness into conscious foresight so that, by integrating the emerging forces into what is vital and forward-looking in our present set-up and discarding the obsolescent and the obsolete, we take a hand in creating the new reality.

No one else but us will create it. It will create itself anyway, out of the myriad intertwinings of our separate activities but it will be the better reality, if we work at making it so. The marketing mnemonic SWOT, which covers strengths, weaknesses, opportunities and threats, comes to mind. Individuals in their groups – and none more so than managers as leaders of their work-groups – have to swot and also position themselves. They have to analyse their strengths and weaknesses, use their weaknesses to advantage to increase their strengths, turn threats into opportunities and position themselves, deliberately and consciously, in the scheme of things they want to bring about.

Swotting and positioning can never be done in isolation. They have always to be done 'in relation': in relation to what is being aimed at and in relation to the physical and human environment in its full complexity. The process of 'relating' by its very nature is dynamic, reciprocal and continuous. The functioning individual does not exist in a vacuum; he or she is not, and never has been in recorded history, an isolated unit. Perhaps the first obsolete idea we have to discard is the artificial dichotomy our arid intellectualism has built between the individual and society.

For some, society is an objective and real entity, something out there, against which individuals are powerless and which therefore has to be responsible for them. For others, at the other end of the spectrum, there is no such thing as society; there are only individuals, each seeking an exclusive self-interest, with a magic 'invisible hand' watching over all and somehow smoothing over relational difficulties. Neither view reflects the facts as we know them.

In terms of our concrete experience, society, for each one of us, is made up of the groups to which we belong: our family, our friends; our work-group, trade union, professional association; our football club, music society. In any one of their groups, individuals have power: by interacting with the others in it and working with them, they can achieve its aims; together, they can evolve new aims, to anticipate changing conditions. It is through active participation in their specific groups that individuals can induce changes in the wider groups – their employing company, government, European community and so on in ever-widening circles – to which they are indirectly, but inalienably, related. Individuals have to realize they have the power to bring about the changes they desire.

As there is no dichotomy between the individual and society, so there is no dichotomy between the enterprise and society, whether that enterprise is the proverbial man-and-his-dog, the small firm, or the transnational corporation. The firm has to swot and position itself and its product or service in the market place. No company is an island just as no man is an island. It is itself, through its activities in the groups with which it is connected – its employees, customers, suppliers, finance providers and so on – part of the wider society with which it is also inevitably related.

Perhaps what is actually new today is the visibility of the relationships and of the interdependence. A Chernobyl disaster affects not only its close physical and human environment but spreads its effects for all to see at the other ends of Europe. What is also new is the immediacy of that interconnectedness and interdependence: the effects of the relationship, sought or unsought, are experienced here and now, not at some distant future which can be conveniently ignored.

As there is no dichotomy between individuals and society, there is also no dichotomy between their particular self-interest and the common interest. We best serve our self-interest by attending to the common interest. It is not a question of putting either above the other. The two are inextricably mixed. The same, of course, applies to the self-interest of the firm and the general common interest. Charles E. Wilson, the one-time president of General Motors is a much-maligned man. He never said 'What is good for General Motors is good for the country' but 'What is good for the country is good for General Motors.' As the world is now becoming in some fundamental aspects the global village, the common interest is not circumscribed by one's own country or one's own political and economic union but spreads to become the universal common interest.

This is not easy to accept, let alone practise, especially for those still steeped in unfettered individualism, or those so short-sighted as to be unable to distinguish between the short and the long run of their best interest or, seeing the distinction, choose the immediate transient benefit at the expense of their long-term interest. Yet, the successful managers of the large corporations who will gain the competitive edge over their competitors will be those wise enough to widen their vision to encompass the general interest, fit their company's interest within that general frame and, through effective action, meet both in the same process.

We also have to decompartmentalize our thinking. We do not have separate political, economic, scientific, psychological or ethical problems. We have human problems, with psychological, economic, political and as many more aspects as you like. A problem cannot be satisfactorily resolved by attending merely to one of its aspects. A business which remains confined to the straitjacket of seeing its prime purpose exclusively as economic is incapable of envisioning its opportunities and its problems in their fullness. It certainly will not be successful over time if, settling the economic aspect, it disclaims responsibility for the others by the stance which says: 'This is not our problem; it is a social problem; let the government deal with it.'

Let us also be careful about the language we use. Let us discard those phrases and terms – rat race, compromise, buying-in people, trade-offs, pay-offs – which in truth degrade our humanity and insidiously permeate our consciousness and affect our ways of behaving. Let us use the words which will convey our aims of involving people in the joint effort and the common endeavour, of coordinating abilities and specialisms, of harmonizing and integrating interests. And if the words are not there to meet the new needs, let us create them; in this direction, I have in the book used gerunds extensively, turning present participles of verbs into nouns to denote the dynamic nature of process or activity. The 'managing' function for example evokes its ongoing and interactive characteristics better than the 'management' function which makes it sound fixed and static.

To the women managers who are reading this book, I extend a plea: 'Please keep your differences; do not push them under the carpet or work at doing away with them.' Our contribution which is unique to us as women is to bring, at every managerial level, our different perceptions, our different ways of looking at the world, of doing things. The large corporation, especially, needs the new and the different to weave them into the fabric of its history and culture and thus make them anew. 'The large corporation needs your difference.'

And also another plea, this time personal: please do not take umbrage at my having used the masculine pronoun throughout. While 'their' is evolving to becoming a neutral singular pronoun, it did not seem apposite in every case; and 'they' could not artificially be substituted for 'he' or 'she' or for the neutral singular noun. I have pluralized as much as possible to reduce the use of 'he' and 'his', and retained the masculine singular form only where essential. I have also limited myself to it, for brevity and to avoid any accusation of sexism. To have used 'he' or 'she' in every case would have been unwieldy; omitting one or the other would have been gender-determinant.

The very fact that a woman manager is writing about a woman management thinker should surely preclude any suggestion of sexist discrimination against women. Not only do I hold that women should be at the highest managerial levels but I also hold that business and other organizations would be better run if more women were actively involved in their decision making.

This book is based on a lifetime's experience in the business field, the first half spent in running my own accountancy practice in the international field, and the second in general management in the retail trade.

When I moved into general management in the large organization, I found my ways of thinking and doing very different from those of my colleagues. If I wanted to find out why something had, or had not, happened, I went directly to that person who had, or had not, done that thing. I built my knowledge by contact with those directly involved, not through layers of intervening supervisors. When I wanted to know how better to satisfy our customers, I did not sit in my office, dreaming up a new game or an exotic prize for them. I arranged for customers' meetings, with set agendas which included items which they themselves had been asked to provide. At meetings, whether local or central, I gave the facts and my views as I knew and felt them, not as it was thought they should be given. All of this was just plain common sense to me.

My ways of doing things were different; so were the questions which aroused my intellectual curiosity: questions about my rights as a manager; about exercising power and authority; about controlling people; about how best to deal with conflict; and so on. I felt that I could not do my job as a manager to my own satisfaction unless I understood the whys and wherefores of these basic questions. For my managerial colleagues, these were non-questions. 'Your rights stem from your appointment; no need for you to worry about all that; you're doing a good job; just get on with it.'

Their assurances, in which the patronizing attitude was clearly discernible, did not assuage my questionings and did not deter me from wanting to satisfy my curiosity. So I went to seminars, re-read the literature and brought myself up to date with management thinking and practice. It was all very interesting but my most rewarding experience was to 'discover' Mary Parker Follett. Unlike the others who illuminated a point here and a point there, Follett gave a comprehensive view of things which encompassed the questions that had been puzzling me. She provided me with satisfying answers to them and, in the process, made me the better manager, and also the better citizen.

Mary Parker Follett (1868–1933) was not only a scholar and a political thinker of depth and integrity but also a woman of vision. Already, in the early 1900s, she grasped the need for the universalistic view and, as a natural by-product, was laying down the fundamentals of integrative, dynamic management. She died before she could put her philosophy of management, mainly given as lectures, into definitive form. However, her lectures were posthumously collected and published under the title of *Dynamic Administration: the Collected Papers of Mary Parker Follett*. A summary of her life and work is given in the appendix and I hope that some readers may be induced to go direct to her writings. Interestingly enough, the Japanese 'discovered' Follett in the early 1960s. They study her writings, put her teachings into practice and have a flourishing Follett Society.

There is today perhaps no more interesting activity than business management. The role of managers extends beyond making the better product, the larger profit and satisfying the customer, essential as these are to good performance. These ends are but part of their main responsibility to build, in the groups in which they operate and which they lead, the creative community. Their work-group is a microcosm of society; the more they make it just and fair, the more its members spread the practice of justice and fairness outwards into those other groups to which they belong; the more managers make their work-groups fun and productive, the more active and effective are its individuals in their outside activities. The creative community of the work-group spills over into the creative groups of the wider society to which it belongs.

This is a great challenge. The way is painstaking, but also exciting and fun and the results gratifying and truly worthwhile. First and foremost, every manager must become conscious of his or her power, and be determined to use it. There is a school of thought which holds that chief executives have to be the begetters of every initiative in the organization; unless any change has their stamp of approval and continued attention, it will not prevail. It seems strange to me that those who give the chief executive exclusive power of effective action, which makes for the undemocratic and authoritarian organization, are the same people who say that the organization is now a network of groups and activities, interdependent and interactive.

Heaping everything on the head of the chief executive is defeatist; it is simply passing the buck. It is in fact the duty of managers to run their work-groups effectively and to introduce and implement in them whatever changes are necessary to that end. Within any constraining parameters, the degrees of freedom are much larger than is usually thought, if only they will seize them. Today, managers can lay the foundations for our better future. They have the power; they need the vision, the understanding and the will to actualize it.

This book, the product of my experience in general management based on Follettian guidelines, is intended to provide managers with a kind of map to show them more clearly the way ahead. I very much hope it meets its purpose.

I

Business in Society: The Creative Connection

Businesspeople are the most potent creators of wealth and of change in society. Yet, generally in Europe and especially in the UK, they are not held in high public esteem; they have no recognized standing in society. If some of 'the great and the good' were invited to a symposium to speculate on social values and the future of society, it is unlikely that businesspeople would be asked to join the gathering and, if they were, the odds are that they would contribute least to their combined counsels.

The main reasons for this are not difficult to pinpoint. On the one side, influential groups in society, out of religious or cultural values, have a tendency to equate wealth with materialism, greed and selfishness; somehow, the suspicion lurks that wealth creation is grubby, disreputable and perhaps somewhat immoral. On the other side, most businesspeople are practical operators who do not go for speculative theorizing, but think from the ground up. They see their role in society merely as a passive one; as controllers of their business enterprises, they take the opportunities open to them and the constraints on their actions as determined by the society in which they operate.

So, society in general does not think sufficiently highly of businesspeople and they, too, greatly underrate their contribution to it and sell themselves short. This is a pity and a loss, for this joint failure deprives them of the standing in society which rightfully should be theirs and deprives society of the fuller contribution they could make, if their role were better understood and appreciated. Artists, scientists, thinkers may succeed in changing the perceptions and ways of looking at the world of their peers and of elite groups, but it is the entrepreneurs who are the people of action. They translate these new insights into actuality for society and, in addition, through their own original contributions, create whole new ranges of goods and services. They are the true wealth creators; and it is the wealth they create that enriches their society and goes to help the poor and the weak.

I find it fascinating that a full-blooded recognition of the value of wealth creation to society should come from a Russian who wrote recently in *Moscow News*, one of the remarkable new *glasnost* generation of Soviet newspapers: 'As a society, we are doomed to poverty as long as wealth is recognized as the highest vice.' Whilst not adopting such extreme views in the West, the tendency here is at best to look down on wealth creation. Aren't the *nouveaux riches* invariably seen as vulgar, and hasn't new money got to go through a couple of generations at least before it becomes respectable?

It is high time, I think, to recognize and spell out the positive contributions of business and wealth creation.

The Role of Business in Society

Some two centuries ago, businesspeople in the UK began to create what was to become the industrial society. Their successors in the industrialized countries this century brought into being the post-industrial society. Today, the present generation is in the process of metamorphosing it into some quite new society – the global society – the shape of which is far from fully discernible at this stage of its development.

Entrepreneurs are above all 'doers' and obviously 'doing' involves change. Everywhere, they are busy adjusting to the evolving situation: reshaping their organizations to meet the requirements of the international markets their enterprise is creating; spreading their manufacturing facilities as required to be near their markets or to circumvent political restrictions; transferring their sourcing as economic opportunity offers; acquiring companies in some countries and entering into alliances or joint ventures in others; creating new forms of capital; new products; new services; innovating in every direction. In the process, they are also changing the mores of the diverse societies in which they operate either as buyers or sellers, manufacturers or capital providers. Yet, they would neither claim nor take the credit for this.

The success of the big corporations in internationalizing their business activities has been truly remarkable. The business leaders in the USA, Europe, Japan and elsewhere have, over the last few decades, been the architects of something approaching a social revolution, well beyond their own boundaries and well beyond the political thinking and the political will of the countries involved. Now, of course, the European Economic Community and the Single Market Act give them a new and major impetus. Increasingly, they are edging us towards the new global age, the one world, where we see and experience our fundamental and proximate interdependence. More than any other group, the managers of the large corporations are building the interactive, interlocking world society. Yet, they would spurn to claim any such intention.

Television and tourism, products of business enterprise, have almost certainly done more than any other single agency to change national outlooks and, to some extent, national characteristics. The social impact of these developments in communications is, if anything, even more widespread than the economic consequences. This is particularly so in those countries whose people do not enjoy the same standard of living as that available in the advanced or more liberal economies. These people, not unnaturally, begin to clamour for a slice of the cake which they see others enjoying in such abundance. Not to be too simplistic about it, this is what happened and is happening in the USSR. The groundswell of public opinion intensified the need for changes in the political system. *Glasnost* and *perestroika*, which have created their own dynamic, the consequences of which are difficult to foresee, came just in time to assuage the pent-up aspirations and expectations of the population. The same grassroots upheaval, moulded by the new means of communication, has been felt in the other countries of the Eastern European bloc, the People's Republic of China and elsewhere in the world.

The commercialization of the birth control pill has, more than anything else, changed the position of women, particularly in Western societies, starting in the family and radiating outwards in changes in demographics, in employment patterns, in legal systems, in social mores.

The applications of information technology are revolutionizing the social scene. They will increasingly change our modes of working, our housing patterns, our transportation needs. At a basic level, they will change the ways in which we, as individuals, connect with each other.

The wide and immediate availability of information and therefore of knowledge, through television set and computer access, will further democratize power which, in its turn, will change the power relations in and between all groups in society, be they the family, the professional association, the trade union, the corporation, the government.

Changes in political systems, in demographics, in the physical environment, in cultural and social mores, today, illustrate some of the effects of business activity on society worldwide. The results of the actions of the individuals running the large business enterprises are there for all to see. Yet, just as Molière's *Bourgeois Gentilhomme* was amazed to learn that he had been speaking prose all his life, so would most business leaders be surprised if told that they are the most effective change-agents in society. They would agree that they have decidedly improved our material conditions, but they would strenuously deny that they are in the business of changing society.

A Unique Business: the John Lewis Partnership

There are, of course, some business leaders who go against the general grain and are both thinkers as well as doers. They know they can, through the way they organize their business, change their immediate society and they go ahead and do it. They develop their own unique philosophy, if necessary codify it and proceed to implement it in their business, both internally and externally. Industrial history offers many examples of such men of vision and action. One who springs immediately to my mind is John Spedan Lewis, for he was the founder of the John Lewis Partnership, a company for which I had the privilege and the pleasure to work for some ten years.

As a young man in the early 1900s, when he entered his father's drapery business in Oxford Street, London, Spedan Lewis was struck by the fact that 'the profit, even after £10,000 had been set aside as interest at 5 per cent on capital, was equal to the whole of the pay of the staff, of whom there were about 300.' Years later, in a BBC broadcast in 1957, Spedan Lewis was explaining:

It was soon clear to me that my father's success had been due to his trying constantly to give very good value to people who wished to exchange their money for his merchandise; but it also became clear to me that the business would have grown further and that my life would have been happier if he had done the same for those who wished to exchange their work for his money.

From this twin realization that it was not fair that the Lewis family, after interest on their capital, received by way of profit as much as the whole staff of 300, and that the business would have grown bigger and also made him happier had his father given very good value to 'those who wished to exchange their work for his money', John Spedan Lewis went on to build the John Lewis Partnership which today has over 16,000 partner–employees, can boast a history of continued financial success and is recognized worldwide as a model of industrial democracy.

The John Lewis Partnership has been thoroughly studied by sociologists and other social scientists. It has a constitution, councils, committees and other devices, all designed to protect the rights of the partners from arbitrary authority, enable them to share knowledge and power and enjoy the profits, after the usual prudent provision for reserves, of their enterprise. All these arrangements have been fully written about, but there is one function which perhaps has not been sufficiently highlighted: that of the registrar. The registrar must always be a *woman* and every trading branch of the John Lewis Partnership (as indeed the various constituencies of the centre) must have one. Although having no executive responsibilities, the registrar stands, in terms of status and authority, equal to the general manager in charge of the branch.

Quite simply, John Spedan Lewis had equated the management of the business with that of the family. Just as in the family, the husband was the go-getter and aggressive breadwinner and the wife the peacemaker and the upholder of the family's conscience, so, Spedan Lewis deduced, it had to be in the business. The general manager was there to make the profits but the registrar, a woman at his side, had to ensure that these were achieved fairly and justly. To enable her to do this, the head of branch has to keep her continuously informed of what's going on from his side and she, in turn, keeps him *au fait* with the intangibles of feeling, tone and morale of the branch. In particular, the registrar has to see that the partners in the branch, each one of whom has direct and confidential access to her, are treated with due consideration and understanding.

The registrar's function is different from the function of the personnel department; in fact, she embodies the conscience of the head of the branch. I used to joke with mine and tell her that, as I was a woman and a head of branch, I combined in myself both the hard and soft attributes of the ideal manager and her role was in my case redundant. It was not of course so. She was actually a tremendous support and comfort, always providing sensitive and wise advice and guidance. She was also more than a 'conscience'. Being in a way outside the hurly-burly of the business side, she was an impartial and disinterested observer and thus a confidante whose business judgement I valued highly. Most other heads of branches similarly valued the contribution their registrar made to the well-being of their branch.

I have always thought this idea of having a 'conscience' well and truly present at the head of a business a most interesting and worthwhile invention. Some may think such a post with all its surrounding trappings either an irrelevant eccentricity or a luxury which only the rich organization could afford. The John Lewis Partnership does not think so, but considers it a necessary cost, essential to enable it to fulfil its aims – of making profits, of course, but always in accordance with the demands of social justice and fairness. The presence of that 'conscience' at the side of the head of branch means that deviations from right behaviour which he or she may be tempted to stray into (and the temptations can be many) are nipped in the bud and almost always entirely avoided.

These days, social audits in a way fulfil a part of this 'conscience' function, but auditing after the event, however useful, is not as effective as preventing the unfairness or the injustice or the wrong-doing being committed in the first instance. When I see the photographs of the boards of directors in the various annual reports which come my way, I sometimes think to myself that it would be nice to see, amongst all these male heads, a woman's face, with, below, her function starkly described as 'our conscience'. No mere token woman director, she, but a doer, ensuring that the men in bringing home the bacon do it according to what is right and just.

For John Spedan Lewis, social goals and economic objectives were closely related, both striving to produce the healthy and successful enterprise and, by extension, the healthy and richer society. He built his Partnership on this basic foundation. It continues to realize in full his vision and his aim.

The Business Ethic

John Spedan Lewis codified his philosophy and over time went on adjusting it, as he evolved in his ideas and as practical requirements demanded. He had to create his own, because there is no specific, written-down business ethic and his, in any case, differed materially from that generally prevailing in his time, and indeed still prevailing today.

Any group of individuals carrying on the same kind of activities develops its own paradigm, the system of values and standards which guides its members in their work and in their relations with others. These values and standards evolve out of practical need and out of the culture of their society, itself the product of many influences. In due course, they can become enshrined, as in the professions, into a specific ethical code which is binding on the members of the group. Most of the professions have gained statutory authority for their activities and, within that framework, establish their own values and standards. There is the medical ethic, the legal ethic and so on.

Businesspeople, as such, have not yet formed themselves into a profession; they have no statutorily recognized body and no formalized business ethic which is binding on them. However, values and standards need not be, and are not always, codified. Scientists, in their various disciplines, have their own unwritten framework of reference within which they operate. Businesspeople, like the scientists, have their philosophy and rules of the game which they believe in and practise in their business dealings.

This business ethic has had a somewhat chequered history. Already, when Colbert was trying to build a manufacturing base for France, around the 1670s, based on strict state regulation, the deputies for commerce had replied, '*laissez-nous faire*' – quite simply telling him to get off their backs and let them get on with it. The phrase '*laissez-faire*' was taken up later by the Physiocrats, the school of political and economic writers which had great influence on Adam Smith, and became the clarion call for free enterprise unfettered by state interference.

The business ethic may be said to have come into its own in the nineteenth century, with the movement away from agriculture in the country to industry in the town, the growth of trades and manufactures and the loosening of the state's grip on the economy. The ethic reflected the stirrings of the age, calling for liberty. It was based on the notion that the individual seeking exclusively his own particular interest and achieving success through his personal striving would *ipso facto* benefit his community and society as a whole, without any such intention on his part – the sociological idea of the Scottish founding fathers of social science, of unintended consequences of intended action. Transferred to the business firm, the individual's success through self-interest and enterprise became the doctrine of competition.

The first conception of this doctrine is attributed to Adam Smith whose book *The Wealth of Nations* was published in 1776. A comprehensive and moral programme based on the study of market forces, it expounded the economic philosophy of 'the obvious and simple system of natural liberty'. General welfare depends on allowing the individual, subject to his not violating 'the laws of justice' to promote his own interest. 'By pursuing his own interests, he frequently promotes that of the society more effectually than when he really intends to promote it. I have never known much good done by those who affected to trade for the public good.'[1]

This then became the business ethic: that business firms be left free to pursue their own self-interest through maximizing their profits and that in this way they would, unintentionally, produce the maximum satisfaction for the community as a whole. Buyers would choose, amongst the goods and services offered by competing firms, those that gave them greatest utility, and the firms which did not produce what the buyers wanted, or produced the desired things at uncompetitive prices, would fail to survive and disappear; only the most effective firms would remain in business and this would be for the benefit of society as a whole. This business ethic, made up of the trinity of self-interest, free enterprise and the market, was, in effect, a mirror image of the individual ethic of the time; it was widely accepted and almost became the spirit of the age of early industrial Britain.

The unfettered workings of the business ethic, leaving it to that 'invisible hand' hovering over the free market to smooth out all difficulties proved in fact not to be universally beneficent; they did not make for the best of all possible worlds; they had to be curbed by continuous government intervention and restrictions. Economic conditions in the first decades of this century made, in due course, for a return of the primacy of the state to take direct control of the economy; in some cases in part, in others in whole. The centralized bureaucratic running of industries failed, in its turn, to produce satisfactory results and, in the Communist countries, the ethic of the state to give priority to social goals over economic objectives failed dismally to improve the standard of living of the people.

The clock has now been turned back full circle. In the UK, it is significant that Samuel Smiles's book *Self-Help*, first published in 1859, the same year as Darwin's *Origin of the Species* and Mill's *Essay on Liberty*, was republished as a Penguin in 1986, with an introduction by Sir Keith Joseph, the then Minister for Education. The book that in its time brought into common usage the maxim 'God helps those who help themselves', celebrating the entrepreneur and the capitalist system, regains favour. Milton Friedman, the American Nobel prizewinner for Economics and the foremost exponent of the free-market economy, forthrightly sets out today the business ethic in the free-enterprise system:

There is one and only one social responsibility of business – to use its resources and engage in activities designed to increase its profits, so long as it stays within the rule of the game, which is to say, engages in open and free competition, without deception or fraud.[2]

And the countries in Eastern Europe and the USSR abandon Communism and return to the business ethic of self-interest working itself out in the *laissez-faire* conditions of the market.

Yet, although there is now a general acceptance of the value of the business ethic, there is still a wide divergence of views about its place in the general scheme of things and of what precisely it should cover. There are church leaders who believe that social goals should always take precedence over economic objectives; enlightened business leaders, who hold that social responsibilities and economic objectives form an integral whole and are not separable; myopic businesspeople who strictly follow the Friedmanite doctrine and consider that social responsibilities are entirely outside their frame of reference and exclusively the province of government; and others who hold different combinations of these three main standpoints.

For my part, I am passionately convinced that the only sustainable business ethic is that which combines moral dictates, social responsibilities and economic objectives and is used as the basic strategy which directs all the activities of the firm.

The Vital Questions

That there should be so many contrary views of the principles which underpin business activity indicates that they need urgent review so that a consensus in the light of current needs be developed and agreed upon. There is in any case for businesspeople and managers a continuous need to rethink the nature and purposes of their business in terms that reflect best current practice and take this forward to meet the emerging needs of the future.

The vital questions are:

- Who is the company?
- What are its ends apart from its trading objectives? What could these ends be?
- To whom are the company and/or its directors responsible?
- Does the pursuit of self-interest mean trampling on others and using questionable means to get one's way?
- Does competition mean deviousness and slyness in out-manoeuvring the opposition?
- Do businesspeople, to be successful, need to live in dread of having to sell their soul?

These are not theoretical questions but of essential and practical importance to those running businesses, especially to those managers and directors in charge of large corporations, where size and distance can blur vision and feeling. Even subconsciously, all executives continuously advert to them.

We outgrow concepts and develop a wider understanding, through experience, of how things can be made to work better; we act in terms of the new logic. But, because of the pull of the past, the tendency is to continue to explain the new experience in terms of the old concepts. Sometimes, we postulate a new concept but, entrapped by the past, give it limited currency, using the wider idea for certain purposes and the old one for others. Creatures of habit, we find it easier to remain within the old frame of reference. Even when the change has been made and we claim to be working under the new reality, the spirit of the old pervades and insidiously subverts our ways of thinking and therefore of behaving. We live in the present and think in the past and sometimes we live and think in the present but talk in the past.

This is very much the case with the business ethic. Far too many business people are still fixated on what Adam Smith is supposed to have decreed it to be over two centuries ago, when he was thinking of the butcher, the baker and the brewer – a very different business world from ours today. Others update their behaviour but not their language and continue to justify their behaviour in terms of obsolete ideas.

The questions go to the root of the business ethic. They need to be exposed, debated and integrated. The present inherent confusions, due to carrying a load of outworn ideas which do not fit coherently with the new conditions, do not help businesspeople to run their companies in the most effective manner; and, accordingly, do not produce the best results for society as a whole.

The Elusive Meaning of Self-interest

As self-interest is at the core of the business ethic, as it is indeed of so much else, it is useful to look at it in some detail.

Self-interest is a basic fact of life. It is one of the fundamental blocks of survival, perhaps *the* basic one. There is no reason therefore to decry it. It is the best springboard to personal and joint endeavours. Because different individuals have different abilities and aspirations, their self-interest is different. The butcher's self-interest is to sell meat at a profit to himself; the scientist's to advance the theory which will bring him renown and the facilities to further his research. If all interests were identical, life would stagnate. It is through the interplay of different self-interests that diversity arises and that progress is made.

Self-interest *demands* cooperation. It could not prosper otherwise. In his fascinating book *The Selfish Gene*, Richard Dawkins, the eminent ethologist, whilst using Tennyson's phrase 'nature red in tooth and claw' to sum up natural selection goes on to say that 'the manufacture of a body is a cooperative venture of such intricacy that it is almost impossible to disentangle the contribution of one gene from that of another.' For Dawkins, the gene has to cooperate and be altruistic in order to achieve its basic selfishness to survive. Given that one is the reciprocal of the other, one could put it the other way round and say that the gene has to be selfish in order to better fulfil its altruism. Be that as it may, it still remains that altruism (effective cooperation) is just as essential as selfishness (aggressive competition) to the gene to forward its self-interest. It could not survive otherwise. In dynamic interaction, cooperation and competition control each other. They are the two sides of the same coin of self-interest.

Over time, our understanding of the nature of personal self-interest has evolved; as we learn that our self-interest is better served by cooperating, so we learn to cooperate. Because of the wider ramifications of its operations, self-interest in the corporation has, over time, evolved even more extensively than in its more simple personal applications.

The corporate self-interest was, to begin with, considered to be synonymous with that of its shareholders, all others being subservient to it. Through trial and error, however, companies have learnt that there can be no such hierarchy of interests. A company has to satisfy the interests of its customers, to gain their loyalty; those of its suppliers to get good service from them; those of its employees since 'a satisfied employee is a satisfied customer'. A company has to retain the confidence of its bankers and financial providers. It must learn to cooperate with its competitors in matters of joint interest. It needs the well-integrated and lively community to provide it with the skilled workforce on the one hand, and its customers on the other; the kind of government that secures the stable and well-ordered environment. It has to value and sustain the favourable public opinion.

At the end of the day, the owners' interest can only be best satisfied, when all the others have been met, and in their proper measure. All sectional interests are found to be interdependent.

The parameters of this self-interest are revealed in the activities of the enlightened and enterprising modern corporation in what is usually considered to be the social field: it lends people to voluntary organizations and to government to help them better run their outfits; it gives money and time to inner-city regeneration schemes; it institutes training schemes for the long-term unemployed; it funds community projects; it establishes scholarships and professorships; it gives to charities, to political parties. New responsibilities have appeared on the scene, such as those of preserving the ozone layer, the rain forests, the environment in its various needs. The self-interest of corporations will be found to be *unending*, continuously evolving out of their increasing and widespread activities.

It is interesting, on this question of self-interest, to contrast and compare the views of Adam Smith and Milton Friedman:

It is not from the benevolence of the butcher, the brewer or the baker, that we expect our dinner, but from their regard to their own interest. We address ourselves, not to their humanity, but their self-love and never talk to them of our own necessities but of their advantage.[3]

Self-interest is not myopic selfishness. It is whatever it is that interests the participants, whatever they value, whatever goals they pursue. The scientist seeking to advance the frontiers of his discipline, the missionary seeking to convert infidels to the true faith, the philanthropist seeking to bring comfort to the needy – all are pursuing their interests, as they see them, as they judge them by their own values.[4]

Whilst Adam Smith's concept of self-interest is specific and clear-cut, that of Milton Friedman's is very wide indeed. The most unselfish act, done without thought of any kind of return can be described as a self-interested act, as defined here by Friedman. What happens presumably is that the individual compares costs and benefits, assesses that the advantage to be derived from his unselfish act – an easy conscience, a better sleep – outweighs the cost involved in its performance and decides as a result to do it. On Friedman's definition of self-interest, Mother Teresa's work in Calcutta, for example, is the expression of her self-interest. This is certainly not the kind of self-interest Adam Smith had in mind or that is commonly understood.

The Social Responsibilities of Business

Friedman goes on to a concept of the social responsibility of business which, to me, seems to be at odds with his ideas on personal self-interest. He holds that business has one and only one social responsibility which is to make the most money for its shareholders; anything else would be highly detrimental to the workings of the free market and therefore to our free society. He is adamant on the subject:

Few trends could so thoroughly undermine the very foundations of our free society as the acceptance by corporate officials of a social responsibility other than to make as much money for their stockholders as possible. This is a fundamentally subversive doctrine.[5]

Friedman's thesis is that directors are elected to manage and increase shareholders' funds. Anything that is done by the corporate executives must be done with that in view. It is not for them to arrogate to themselves the responsibility of assessing the worthiness of social causes and use company funds, the inalienable property of the shareholders, to pursue social goals. He holds that such expenditure, if incurred, is *ultra vires* the authority of the officials, and shareholders could successfully sue for misappropriation of funds. So far, despite the lavish spending by American companies on what is considered to be social causes and the love of litigation in that country, no shareholder there has yet attempted to prove his point.

Friedman not only holds that corporate executives are not entitled to use company monies for social ends but also considers that they are incapable of effective decision making in such matters:

If businessmen do have a social responsibility other than making maximum profits for stockholders, how are they to know what it is? Can self-selected private individuals decide what the social interest is? Can they decide how great a burden they are justified in placing on themselves or their stockholders to serve that interest?[6]

His robust views caused considerable controversy. The debate rages on, with academics and others taking up the challenge, in journals and books on management, ethics, and associated subjects, in the USA and elsewhere, mostly to argue against his forthright tenets. One hesitates to enter the fray but the whole thing is surely a non-debate. It is that word 'social' which is the bone of contention and which for Friedman seems to mean the company taking over the work of government.

As corporate executives are fully entitled to spend whatever they consider necessary to progress their shareholders' interest, it is right and proper for them to contribute money and other resources to help create the milieu in which the business can prosper and fructify. If directors had any doubt as to the propriety of expenditure deemed 'social', they could easily ask their shareholders to find out whether they approve of it or not. In West Germany, company chairpersons already devote part of their annual report to explaining how much of their shareholders' money they have spent on cleaning the environment: 'and that is the part that gets the loudest applause from the shareholders' (*Economist*, 15 April 1989). Directors are not worried today about their right to spend on 'social' endeavours or even whether they can afford it. The question which they now put to themselves is: 'Can we afford *not* to do this?'

The full answer, of course, to Friedman's concern is that there is no divergence, no conflict of purpose in the long run between the self-interest of the business and the general social interest; a long run which is becoming very short indeed. It is one and the same. The business enterprise is an economic organization and also at the same time a social agency. Its economic purpose simply cannot be cut off from its other purposes, social, political and so on, which it actually fulfils.

Over seventy years ago, Follett was already considering the question and answering it loud and clear:

We cannot departmentalize our thinking . . . We cannot think of economic principles and ethical principles . . . I do not think we have psychological and ethical and economic problems. We have human problems with psychological, ethical and economic aspects, and as many more as you like, legal often.[7]

Running a business is not a mathematical exercise, where sums and equations can be right or wrong, never good or bad. Economic activity is a human endeavour and thus includes all the facets that actuate human behaviour. In decision making, every manager has to take account of all these aspects; leaving any one of them out, whether it be the legal or the ethical, the political or the psychological, makes for the wrong and the bad decision.

As to whether the corporate executives – self-selected private individuals as Friedman, interestingly, calls them – can fathom out and decide what the social responsibilities of the company are, the answer must surely be 'yes'. When a perceived social obligation or interest is identified as a matter of corporate self-interest, there is no one better qualified to make the judgement and institute the action than the businesspeople involved. The best of them already do it. But not all have the breadth of vision to perceive the self-interest of the business in its fullness.

Big Business: the New Leviathan

Businesspeople know, perhaps better than anyone else, that the trend towards big business is unlikely to go away, at least in the foreseeable future. They are creating and actualizing the trend. They have been its progenitors and its own dynamic will now take it forward and make it grow. As trade barriers between countries are dismantled, and we still have to see the long-term effects of the single European market after 1992, the movement will gain an even greater impetus. As we move effectively towards the globalization of markets, the need to gain critical mass in market share will lead to fierce competition and/or combination, leaving in many industries a small number of very large world players. This does not mean that there will not be growth in small and medium-sized businesses. These will prosper by satisfying local demand, exploiting niche markets and providing personal services which the larger corporations, in their massive and impersonal organizations, are unlikely to be able to offer.

The powers accumulated in the hands of the men and women managing the global corporations will be immense. Already, there are some companies with larger budgets than those of fair-sized independent countries. And through their worldwide activities, their influence will be spread worldwide. Powerful, they will yet be subjected to the scrutiny and the audit of an increasingly sophistic-ated and socially concerned society, similarly spread worldwide, able to mobilize world opinion and action against the corporation which it feels is behaving irresponsibly in one way or another.

There has already been a shift of popular feeling against big business. Until recently, in the UK, it was on the whole respected, admired and very often fêted. Now, there are clear indications that the pro-business honeymoon is over.

In the USA, which is invariably the harbinger of things to come, Nader, the great consumerist campaigner of the 1960s, working almost single-handedly, got Californian voters in November 1988 to vote 'yes' to a referendum proposition that the car insurers should cut their premiums by 20 per cent, without doing anything to change the state's legal system which, by increasing the size of the compensation awards, had caused the increase in premiums in the first place. Most people thought the courts would say this was illegal, but California's Supreme Court ratified the vote a few months later. Share prices of insurance companies including many British ones, operating not only in California but in the USA generally, came down immediately with a bump in response.

The environmental questions will come uppermost. In the USA, corporations are now endeavouring to reduce the deleterious effects of their manufacturing activities on the environment. In Europe, companies in Scandinavia and West Germany have been in the forefront in taking corrective action and those in the other countries are waiting for governmental and EC legislation to compel them to clean up as they go.

This upsurge against big business is inevitable. The occasional disaster is likely to be the big disaster which will label the company involved in it 'Big Company Wrecks World' (*Economist*, 15 April 1989) and the indictment is unlikely to be restricted to one isolated company.

The Social Trends in the 1990s

The social trends forecast for the 1990s include a more altruistic society, away from the period of selfism when people were largely concerned with seeking only their own satisfactions to a period when they will be more concerned for others and especially those in need. There will be some return to government intervention, due to the need to take concerted, international action regarding the environment, but governments will have to be seen to be efficient. This acceptance of collectivism will be allied with a greater desire for more individual personal choice. Individual responsibility plus collective efficiency is likely to be the model for the next decade, as well as a desire for greater egalitarianism, spreading over the whole political spectrum. The majority of rich and relatively rich people, for example, appears to be prepared to pay more in tax to alleviate poverty. Open citizenship – a strong feeling for one's own country combined with respect and feeling for the values of other nations – is another emerging trend. The feeling of empathy with and solidarity with others, in less fortunate conditions whether in one's country or elsewhere, will become more pronounced. Ethical watchdogs will abound. This is the probable environment in which companies will be operating.

In May 1989, *The Ethical Consumer* published, in its UK edition, a plan for a worldwide campaign against Nestlé. Following a renewed American campaign on the baby milk issue, a boycott of Nestlé products was officially launched in the UK, to be supported by consumers in Germany, France, Austria, Scandinavia and some twelve other countries. The issue was Nestlé's alleged use of unethical marketing promotion techniques in the Third World, in giving away free samples of infant formula powdered milk to new mothers, as they left the maternity wards. This powdered milk, because of the lack of clean water with which to make up the formula, leads to the baby-bottle disease from which, it is said, a baby dies every three minutes somewhere in those countries.

What is significant is that, whilst the boycott was to be specifically directed against buying Nescafé (which has about half the market in instant coffee in the UK, worth some £300 million a year), it was not limited to it. All of Nestlé's products, defined as those belonging to companies wholly or partially owned by Nestlé, were also to be shunned. There were 112 branded items which the conscientious protester had to avoid; and these did not include those of l'Oréal, the biggest cosmetics manufacturer in the world which, being 28 per cent owned by Nestlé, 'thus receives Nestlé's record as well' and got black marks under almost every count, in another section of the magazine.

Actions underpinned by this sort of organization can no longer be considered the exclusive concern of small and unimportant fringes. Without the promptings of *The Ethical Consumer*, the Rowntree Charitable Trust, to take one example, is said to have decided to sell its holding in Rowntree, when the company was taken over by Nestlé, because of the baby milk issue. There are already five 'no-go areas' in which ethical funds will not invest: alcohol, tobacco, armaments, gambling and South Africa. This trend will become more pronounced in the 1990s, appealing to wide sections of society and campaigns will be aimed directly at reducing the profits of the targeted companies.

All the signs indicate that, in the 1990s, big business will get bigger still, but it will be working under conditions of much greater transparency than today. The men and women in charge of operations will have to hold themselves accountable not only to their shareholders but much more so to articulate and committed groups from unexpected and unpredictable corners who know how to gather information and how to use it to mould public opinion.

Corporation Ethics and the Business Ethic

Business ethics has been a growth industry in the USA since the 1970s. It is a subject now taught in over five hundred courses across the country's colleges and universities and in most business schools. It was not being taught at the Harvard Business School and suggestions have been made that this could have been a contributory factor to Boesky, the disgraced 1988 arbitrageur and one of Harvard's alumni, proclaiming in 1985 to students at the University of California: 'Greed is all right, by the way. I want you to know that. I think that greed is healthy. You can be greedy and still feel good about it.' The Harvard Business School is remedying its omission. It accepted the £30 million pledge by the ex-chairman of the Securities and Exchange Commission to incorporate business ethics in its curriculum and convince students that 'ethics pays' (*Fortune*, 1987).

Reading the credos and ethical policy statements of some of the American companies leaves one quite amazed. Corporations are taking upon themselves so many responsibilities as to make one wonder whether they can effectively implement them; ethical corporate structures are being put in place, with training workshops in ethics, ethical audits, ethical programme evaluations and a host of other similar measures. In their codes of practice, companies are now putting their first responsibility to the customer, then to the employee, then to the community and finally to the shareholder.

Constraints imposed upon employees strain credibility and feasibility. The *Washington Post*, for example, in its 1989 Code of Standards and Ethics requires that, apart from the obligatory 'we pay our way' and no freebies of any kind being allowed, their journalists' political activity be limited to voting only and that neither they nor their families be involved in any partisan cause (*Sunday Times*, 1 October 1989). It is a little startling to find that one's spouse and one's children have to be banned from political activity, simply because they are members of a journalist's family.

To me, one gratifying thing to read is that, in the questionnaires administered to MBA students to analyse their ethical attitudes through their responses to business dilemmas, the women students are being found to hold a much stricter sense of right and wrong. As more and more women move into managerial positions, this augurs well for the future, in terms of their own behaviour and their influence on that of their male colleagues.

Most of the business women leaders in the UK can of course be seen to follow their own personal high ethical standards. Early on in her Welsh factories Laura Ashley established model conditions and facilities for the company's workers, whilst others are still pondering upon their costs. Anita Roddick, of the Body Shop, initiated in 1989, a country-wide campaign to save the rain forests; her first step was to withdraw all merchandise from the shop windows and to display in them instead a stark red poster protesting against deforestation, a brave thing indeed for a retailer to do.

In the UK, companies like the John Lewis Partnership, have had their principles and rules of operation laid down for many years. One of the Partnership's useful rules, for example, is that no partner is allowed to receive gifts or other similar perks from any source; it makes it easier to return the present sent at Christmas by the new supplier who may have forgotten one of the terms of his contract.

I found the rule very helpful to me right at the beginning of my career in the Partnership. The training for general management was rigorous and intense and for me lasted some six months. To begin with, after the initial indoctrination, I had to work for some weeks as a sales assistant and I was sent to an electrical department for the purpose; truly harrowing work for me as I knew nothing about electrical fittings, and packing has never been one of my strong points. Still, one day, a satisfied customer gave me a shilling tip. I was most embarrassed; then, I remembered the Partnership's rule and could tactfully return it by invoking it.

Other companies have their principles so embedded in their culture and ways of conduct that they would consider it unnecessary to put them down on paper. Still, the trend is setting in. The Institute of Business Ethics was established in London in 1987; what would appear to be the first course on business ethics was offered in the same year to Masters students at the London Business School; a Business Ethics Research Centre was established at King's College, London; and a number of other business schools at universities and polytechnics are teaching the subject. At company level, many companies have created, or are creating, codes of ethics, standards of conduct, or similarly inspired regulations.

These codes, when sensible and when followed by managers at all levels, are extremely useful in defining the framework of reference within which all employees can work that more securely – when they know what is, and what is not, acceptable. If it is the rule of the company for employees not to accept gifts, it is easier for them to refuse them; if it is the rule for the company to pay all its suppliers on time, it will not be able to discriminate against its small suppliers, as many a large company currently does; and so on. However, where not followed by all managers, they are counter-productive. Mere 'veneering' will not do; everyone sees it for what it is. It merely breeds cynicism inside the company, making it lose standing generally and provides valuable weaponry to the hostile outside group. Investigative journalism in the media and investigative action by the committed group make corporate behaviour transparent indeed.

Despite all these standards and codes of behaviour and corporation vows, scandals, arising out of questionable or outright unlawful practices, continue to erupt in the business world everywhere. Why is this so? Apart from the old Adam in man, there is little doubt, in my mind, about their underlying cause. It is because the new codes and standards are being superimposed on a still firmly held business ethic which is at odds with them. All these protestations of responsibilities to customers, employees, community and society do not fit well, do not cohere with the basic message of the business ethic, which still includes a very restricted understanding of the concept of self-interest. The broader responsibilities of companies, although accepted and implemented by the best business leaders as integral elements of their corporate self-interest, are essentially alien to the business ethic as generally understood and exercised; more than that, they are contrary to it.

Updating of the Business Ethic

What is required therefore is not a proliferation of ethical declarations but an updating of the business ethic itself: a full review which goes right down to basics, looks at the business ethic completely anew and comes up with a new version, more in keeping with current reality. After all, the business ethic was not handed down in tablets of stone. It can, and must, be developed. It cannot be limited exclusively to economic ends, to the company making as much money as possible for its shareholders, and nothing else. There is no such thing in life as watertight compartments separately labelled 'political', 'economic', 'social', 'ethical' and so on. A business cannot be abstracted exclusively into an economic entity. Its activities are predominantly economic but they have never been, and can never be, exclusively so. All the other aspects of human behaviour – political, psychological, social, moral and so on – enter into the activities of any business and must all be fully recognized.

The new business ethic must incorporate those broad responsibilities which our more thoughtful and successful businesspeople already take on board, as a matter of course. After all, business leaders do not want to be remembered solely by the financial success of their operations but also for the tangible and intangible benefits their company spreads to the community at large, as a feature of its business activities.

The large corporations in the modern world are truly a new type of species. Their powers are all-pervading. The people leading them are actually shaping society. The best of them, by leading the companies well, are very directly creating the better-ordered and more just society. It would make for clarity, for less ambiguity, for better sense if the much more sophisticated view they take of self-interest becomes a recognized part of the business ethic itself. They are the people best placed to do it. Having created the new paradigms, they can declare and codify them. This would formalize matters and generalize acceptance by the more timorous and the less far-sighted amongst them.

Laws have been enacted from time to time not only in the Companies Acts but in numerous other acts to make companies and directors liable for certain misfeasances and other matters. But the questions posed earlier – who is the company, what are its full responsibilities, to whom are the company and/or its directors answerable and so on – have not yet been fully considered. Some of the questions may need legal clarification, in at least some respects.

In the meantime, they remain amongst the fundamental questions which business leaders and managers themselves have to answer in full. Only a root-and-branch review of the business ethic which recognizes private enterprise as one of the building-blocks of democratic society and therefore accepts in full its concomitant responsibilities to it can provide the modern and coherent framework and the values within which directors and managers can work with certainty and therefore that more effectively.

More urgently than ever, business leaders and managers have to get down to the fundamentals, think through what they are in business for, define and proclaim their true and full role in society and, thus strengthened, go confidently forward to fulfil it.

And their function includes understanding and satisfying the needs of the employees, the people who make the business, the subject which is dealt with in the following chapter.

Notes

1 Adam Smith, *The Wealth of Nations*, Methuen & Co., London, 1776 vol. I, p. 421.
2 Milton Friedman, *Capitalism and Freedom*, Chicago University Press, Chicago, 1962, p. 133.
3 Adam Smith, *The Wealth of Nations*, p. 16.
4 Milton and Rose Friedman, *Free To Choose*, Pelican Books, London, 1980, p. 47.
5 Friedman, *Capitalism and Freedom*, p. 133.
6 Friedman, *Capitalism and Freedom*, p. 133.
7 Mary Parker Follett, *Dynamic Administration: the Collected Papers of Mary Parker Follett*, Elliott M. Fox and L. Urwick, eds., Pitman Publishing, London, 1973, pp. 148–9.

2

People at Work: The Group Factor

It is now widely recognized by enlightened managements that the success or failure of a business enterprise is fundamentally and finally dependent upon its people and how they are used. Managing well the human resource has top priority in the company's objectives and forms an integral part of its business strategy.

Over the years, views have evolved on how to get the most out of people. It is not so very long ago that workers were described as 'hands' and the successful manager was of the 'I command, you do as I say' stereotype. Attitudes have changed and the new notion that has taken root and is likely to spread is that of the manager as the leader of a team. 'Let us work together to get the best results' is the model for the modern manager.

Managers today cohere the staff they manage into the efficient and effective team which fulfils its changing task, always improving performance. Their function is to organize the activities of the individuals in their group in such a way as to mobilize the full energy and initiative of each and integrate them into the joint effort.

The emphasis has moved from getting, by order, the most out of individuals to that of creating the conditions in which they, as parts of the group and of their own volition, will want to give of their best. The new managerial mode requires changes in perception and a subtle understanding of the dynamics involved in group-work.

Individuals in Their Groups

It is only recently that it has come to be generally appreciated that the individual does not operate as an isolated unit, but as part of a group, of a system of interrelating members.

Follett was amongst the first to place individuals in the complex of relationships within the groups to which they belong or which they may join: their family, friends, trade union, professional association, work-group and so on. The unit of society, Follett insisted, is not the individual in isolation. The assumption that a man or a woman thinks, feels and judges independently of outside influences is arid intellectualism which does not accord with the facts. There is no such thing as a separate ego, no such thing as an individual defined as a self-contained unit, with a separate independent existence of its own. Individuals in this absolute sense are nowhere to be found in nature or society. Individuals derive their identity by relating with, and distinguishing themselves from, the others in their various groups. The unit of society is the group-individual.

This does not reduce them to the status of a mere cog in a machine. On the contrary, it is through participating actively in their groups that individuals actualize their potentialities, become fully themselves. And the more and diverse the groups they belong to, the more they develop, the more they grow in understanding and effectiveness. This is extremely important: compare the person who is solely interested in his work and trade union or professional association with the person who, in addition, is also interested in music or the church. The views and attitudes of the former will be more limited, more tunnel-visioned than those of the second individual; his will be more balanced and broader, tempered as they will be by the import of the extra interests of music or church. The trade unionist who is, at the same time, a shareholder and a house-owner will not be, cannot be, as dogmatic in his views as a colleague who is neither of these things. His wider interests impinge upon each other and combine to give him a more rounded outlook.

A great deal is written about society. Some hold that there is no such thing as society, an abstract concept of no material value, but a collection of individuals, each following his interests and aspirations. Whilst it is true that the individual cannot connect with society, there being nothing out there to connect with, he nevertheless does not find himself on his own in a vacuum. He does connect. He connects with other individuals in his specific groups. For the individual, his society is made up of the groups of which he is a member. These groups are very real to him, and also necessary. Without his society, being the constellation of his groups, he could not operate. From this it follows that the wider society is not made up of isolated individuals, but of groups of individuals; and the individual exercises his influence on that wider entity through his activity in his groups. The group mediates individual and society. Follett saw this very clearly:

there is no 'society' thought of vaguely as the mass of people we see around us. I am always in relation not to 'society' but to some concrete group. When do we ever as a matter of fact think of 'society'? Are we not always thinking of our part in our board of directors or college faculty . . . in our football team, our club, our political party, our trade-union, our church? Practically 'society' is for every one of us a number of groups . . . The vital relation of the individual is through his groups; they are the potent factors in shaping our lives.[1]

Individuals affect the others in their groups and are reciprocally affected by them. The dynamic is the same in any group, whether it be the family in session or an international conference of heads of state. Examples could be culled from any group but it is more relevant to use here those which are of common experience in work situations.

When a new managing director or department manager is appointed, the performance of the company as a whole or of that department, more or less quickly, changes. The change flows from the different interactions set in motion by the new member. Moreover, the change does not occur only with a new managerial appointment. A new telephonist, for example, may be better able to make intelligent connections and the company may gain therefore an important customer, one perhaps who might have been put off by the previous exchange delays. To take another example, say a cleaner of an office, the influence of a new person, less careful and more slap-dash than his predecessor, will be immediately felt in the lowered efficiency of the others in that office.

The absence of a member of the group will be felt, for good or bad, in some way, by the whole group. This was well illustrated in a case within my own experience. The directors of a small company with which I was associated all tended to be volatile and tempestuous, except one who somehow could smooth away any number of ruffled feathers and induce a general atmosphere of common sense. When he was away, the board meetings were chaotic with the company secretary hardly knowing what had been, or had not been, decided. We got over that by craftily making sure that there was no necessity to hold a board meeting on any day on which he was likely to be absent.

Such ploys pay off. Follett stressed that, through observation and experiment, we can learn how individuals, as group-individuals, interact with each other and that such knowledge would lead to smoother and more comprehensive interactions, allowing the work-group as a whole to operate more effectively, both qualitatively and quantitatively. The dynamic of the group process – the reciprocal interactions going on between its members – constitutes the creative factor in any group enterprise.

As far back as 1918, Follett was advocating effective group organization as the basis for real democracy in the political field. She used the same concept – effective group organization – for best performance in the work-place. She studied groups in action, as she observed their workings in the varied activities in which she was involved and also in specific sessions with academic and business friends, similarly interested. Her conclusion was that effective relatings, through early and continuous coordination, form the basis of successful group-work.

Since then, work on group dynamics has been carried out mostly in the USA, and has been gathering pace in the last twenty years. The success of Japanese companies, largely built on the basis of effective group-work, has also tended to concentrate the minds of industrialists in the West on this more productive mode of working.

If Follett was among the first to think of industrial and business organization in terms of the work-group, she has certainly not been the last. Much more than the individual, it is the group which is becoming the basic unit of study. For me, familiar with Follett's writings, it is almost uncanny to see the parallelism between current thinking and findings with what she was writing some seventy years ago.

Group Fundamentals

Man did not invent the group. Group formation is a common and characteristic phenomenon through the animal kingdom: the shoal, the pack, the flock, the herd are examples of animal group formations. But it is man who has brought the group to its present levels of importance and effectiveness in civilized society.

Human groups form naturally or by consent. The essential ingredient is the recognized, or tacitly understood, interdependence of its members, flowing from their personal interests which can be better satisfied through combining with others having similar ends. The family is the natural human group but it is not the only group into which a person is born. Other groups overlap with it and themselves. Sex, race, religion, class, climate and geography are some of the other determinants of the larger natural groupings.

Membership of other groups is determined by choice or necessity or a combination of both. The reasons individuals join particular groups, music society, golf club, employing company, are matters of fact that are personal to themselves. One individual joins the golf club through choice, because he enjoys the game; another, a bank manager who heartily dislikes it, joins the club to enlarge his range of customer-contacts. Individuals join, whatever their reason or mixture of reasons, because the balance of advantage as they see it lies in their doing so. And the particular group accepts them because it is also to its advantage. There is always a mutuality of interest, even though it may not always be exactly symmetrical.

When this mutuality disappears, the link is severed. The individual who is working for a company providing high pay but boring work will move to the company which offers high pay plus more exciting work. Conversely, the company will get rid of him, subject to the constraints of its own or outside regulations, when it finds it is not getting value for money from that employee.

The group is a dynamic entity, continuously creating itself anew. It is an open system, also interacting with its outside environment. A company, perhaps through success, may grow complacent and arrogant, thinking it has made itself unbeatable and has permanently assured its future. But danger – the appearance of a competitor, the loss of an important customer, the defection of a valued member to a rival group – immediately sets the alarm bells ringing and galvanizes its members into taking stock and implementing corrective measures, that is if they have not gone too far down the line into unshakable apathy.

Group Types

Groups are categorized, in the main, by a combination of intent, size and form of organization.

A young man and woman going out together and less and less with others are beginning to form a group; so do two or more persons who work together on an *ad hoc* basis. This is the emerging or quasi-group. When that young couple marries or decides to cohabit together, it becomes a functional group, as do those individuals who decide to work more permanently together and form themselves into a partnership or a company.

The relations between the members, small in number, of the functional group, are direct, relatively simple and mutually understood. There is no need to spell them out in detail. Members know what their contribution is to the whole task and their responsibility to the other members of the group. As relations become more complex, they will be informally recorded in writing. The working mother, who leaves a detailed list stuck on the refrigerator door, of who is to do what, is organizing the work for clarity and mutuality of action, that is for best effectiveness. John is to do the hoovering and Jane the shopping. When John finds out that his sister will be late, won't be able to do the shopping and there is nothing to eat for dinner, he will substitute for her, doing the shopping in addition to his hoovering or, if there is no time, do the shopping only, as the more important priority.

There is mutual trust, each member in the functional group trusting that his contribution will be reciprocated by that of the others and, if need be, that they will make up for his occasional inability to do his own bit. This trust is backed by reciprocal control, each member knowing that what he does or does not do is clearly visible to the others, and that any shirking will be met first with disapproval, then with censure and finally perhaps with expulsion from the group. The group will break up, when its members no longer have common interests they want to pursue together, or when their relations deteriorate to the point that cooperation is not possible between them. In the natural group of the family, there will be divorce when husband and wife no longer have a commonality of interests both want to pursue together. The same happens in the small business, when the partners or shareholders find themselves at odds with each other and unable to cooperate.

When the small functional group prospers and grows, the time comes when the direct informal arrangements are no longer enough for efficient operation. The informal relations have to be formalized. Specific tasks, obligations, activities and rights have to be codified in a set of rules. The functional group becomes now the organized group. The need now arises to create an organizing, a managing function: the function to steer, regulate and coordinate all the activities of the group in the way that is best to implement its objectives, whatever these may be.

A business enterprise is an organized group. Many of the largest companies started as associations between a very small number of people. As the business prospered, they had to engage more people and organize the work on the basis of specialisms and in manageable proportions; to devise the form of organization best suited for their activities and strategy and the technology they had; to alter it in anticipation of, or in response to, changes in the environment. Tomorrow's large enterprises are being founded today by entrepreneurs who, on their own or with a friend or two, have an idea which they successfully commercialize.

There is a natural progression, if all goes well, in the quasi-group becoming the functional group and finally graduating into the organized group of increasing complexity, when the entity, say the large international company, becomes a grouping of groups. Because of the difference in size, the large corporation will be differently organized from the small business run from home or small office. Their underlying fundamentals, however, remain the same. Both the international corporation and the small enterprise are founded on the bases of the mutuality of interests, the interdependence and the cooperation of their members. To the extent that any group forgets this, that a member or section of it puts his or its own interest above that of the others, the overall performance of the group suffers, to the detriment of all.

Within this broad categorization of functional and organized groups which are on a more or less permanent footing, variants appear. An important one is the group of a temporary nature, formed to fulfil a specific end, the members of which disband on its completion. Bob Geldof's 'Live Aid' concert was a huge group endeavour, of people coming and working together on a one-off job; passengers, injured in, say, an air crash, join together into a group to make common cause against the airline over compensation issues. In the work-place, different specialists join together to form the project team or the task force to study a particular problem or opportunity, and return to their normal duties, at the end of the assignment. This type of work-group is bound to grow, given the interlocking coordination required between various disciplines, in the complex business activities of today.

The Growth and Growth of Groups

The proliferation of groups has been one of the more noticeable features of post-war society. Both functional and organized groups abound and show no sign of overflow. There are various reasons for this. More can be achieved through group-work: the neighbourhood watch, the residents' association, the pressure group, and so on form because their members realize the strength that comes from uniting. There is also the therapeutic value of the group: Weight Watchers, Alcoholics Anonymous and supportive groups of every kind – now the norm – give their members the knowledge they are not alone in their predicament and the benefit of joining forces for mutual help and corrective reciprocal reinforcement.

Differentiation and segmentation in niche marketing have been, and will no doubt continue to be, important factors in group creation. By identifying people with similar needs or interests and setting out specifically to meet them, marketers are creating new groups all the time. The leisure industry has been built on the group concept which it continues to use with ever-increasing ingenuity. The building industry, following demographic changes, is creating for itself new opportunities by building estates for the elderly. In the process, it is also creating new groups, of the elderly people who can now, because of their proximity to each other, join together and organize themselves to promote their common interest – something they could not do previously, when they were scattered throughout the community, unknown to each other.

This rash in the growth of groups is by no means confined to the UK or to Europe. In Japan, the group activity is endemic to the society. Anyone there doing anything on his own causes utmost surprise. 'Where is your group?' is the standard question to the lone traveller. In the USA, too, the land of the individualist, the growth in the number and variety of groups has been phenomenal.

The growth and speed of modern communications will increasingly lead to the internationalization of groups of all kinds, providing companies with opportunities, in terms of larger customer-segments, for example, but also problems, as the well-organized international pressure group focuses on the company with whose activities it disagrees. The large corporation in particular has to be watchful of this evolving trend and anticipate, in order to avoid, the problems.

Inter-group Relations

The essence of all successful group working is cooperation. Relations of the individuals within the group and between sub-groups forming the overall entity – intra-group relations – will be based, *grosso modo*, on cooperation. Cooperation does not mean always the pleasant spectacle of the parties walking peacefully hand in hand all the way. Over time, individual interests change. There can be many different views on how best to deal with new situations, but differences or conflict in the healthy group, when they arise, will be resolved in the main on the basis of mutual accommodation.

What about relations of the group as an entity with its outside groups in the milieu in which it operates – its inter-group relations? These can be anywhere along a continuum, going from cooperation at one end to competition at the other. Where the relations will fall depends upon how the groups perceive their respective goals. If they think they can achieve their own objectives better by joining in all or some of their activities, they will cooperate on these; if they perceive that their goals are mutually exclusive, they will compete, fighting to gain their own end which they can only get at the expense of the others. Competition, for example, between two suppliers each wanting the same order, or two religious groups each wanting to achieve supremacy is a sufficient cause for conflict. They can change strategies. The 'If you can't beat them, join them' line of action shows the complete move from competition to cooperation, where the latter is seen as the better alternative to securing one's interest.

The closer the connection, the closer is the degree of interdependence, irrespective of whether the link comes to be voluntarily, or involuntarily, established. Manufacturers in the UK can afford to ignore their counterparts in the Far East when the latter are servicing their domestic market only, but they cannot ignore these producers, once they start to sell a better-value product than theirs in the UK. The relationship comes about through no action of theirs but, once there, they have to act to protect their position. What actions they then take depend on the way they view the new situation in which they find themselves and what will serve them best: to compete or cooperate, or anything in between.

Cooperative and Competitive Relations

It is worthwhile looking at the effects of these alternative relations. A considerable amount of research has been done to compare and contrast the behaviour of connecting groups, at the extremities of the continuum; as most of it is carried out in the closed system of the laboratory method, it cannot reliably reflect what would happen in the real world. However, a series of experiments[2] devised to create natural conditions, was carried out in the field. The first and most comprehensive of their kind, the experiments laid the foundations of subsequent research. The findings, validated by later experiments with different groups and in different conditions and cultures, are revealing.

The experiments covered 11- to 12-year-old schoolboys, of similar educational attainment and all coming from the same stable background of American middle-class, white Protestant families. They were carried out in summer camps, the boys not having known each other beforehand and not knowing that they were being studied.

The experiments went through the sequence of group formation (sorting the boys into two separate groups), inter-group conflict creation (a tournament of games with prizes only for the winners) and finally cooperative integration (engineering a superordinate interest, by way of a breakdown in the water supply system).

The tournament started in a spirit of good sportsmanship, but this quickly evaporated. The customary cheer of '2–4–6–8 – Who do we appreciate?' became '2–4–6–8 – Who do we apprecihate?' The rival groups planned raids; a banner left behind by one group was burnt by the other and this seemed like the declaration of war, with hostilities flaring between the two groups. If an outside observer had entered the situation at this point, he could only have concluded, on the basis of their behaviour, that these boys, who actually were la crème de la crème in their communities, were 'wicked, disturbed and vicious bunches of youngsters'. Indeed, one set of experiments had to be abandoned because of the uncontrollable rise in inter-group hostility.

Another effect of the inter-group conflict was the increase in solidarity within each group, all working together against the other.

In-group cooperativeness was highest at the peak of inter-group conflict. The conflict also produced changes in the statuses and role relationships between the individuals in each group. In one group leadership changed hands when the leader who had emerged in group-formation proved reluctant to take front-line action; in the other, the bully became a hero.

Subsequently, more cooperative situations were created: eating in the same dining room; going to the cinema together; setting off fireworks on 4 July. These situations became occasions for the rival groups to display their mutual hostility, the meal-time encounters being dubbed 'garbage-wars' by the participants. Nevertheless, the foundations for joint activity were being laid. Later, the breakdown in the water supply was engineered. The flow of water was interrupted and the boys of both groups were called to hear of the crisis which equally affected them both. They promptly volunteered in their own distinctive ways. They explored first separately and then together how they could repair the trouble; together, they located the source of the difficulty.

Still, despite the good spirits engendered, the two groups fell back on their old recriminations once the immediate crisis was over. Other cooperative exercises were introduced. Both groups separately wanted to go to the cinema but were told the camp could not afford to pay for it. The two groups got together, worked out how much each group would have to contribute, chose the film and enjoyed it together. Then, they went for an outing together and the truck carrying the food was made not to start. The boys got a rope and all pulled together to start it. Joint efforts did not immediately dispel hostility but, gradually, the series of cooperative activities reduced conflict and created mutual friendly acceptance. Table 2.1 shows the different effects of cooperation and competition on two interacting groups.

Cooperation can be seen clearly to lead to better results, both quantitatively and qualitatively. In the cooperating groups, individuals know enough about each other's work to be able to move from one to the other, to help in an emergency. The relations between the two groups, based on trust, are open and truthful, making for fruitful communication. They perceive each other's actions in a positive light and will offer each other truthful suggestions and advice. Members in one group will view those in the other as friendly, willing and adaptable. They will work together to achieve their common and

Table 2.1 Effects on two related groups of cooperation and competition

	Cooperation	Competition
Substitutability	Individuals will substitute for each other to achieve goal.	There will be separate efforts to wrest goal from the other party.
Inducibility	Mutuality; good faith.	Division; conflict.
Communication	Full; open; truthful.	Unreliable; misleading; limited; impoverished.
Perception	Positive; open; flexible.	Poor; divergent.
Task orientation	Joint effort.	Imposed by the stronger upon the weaker party.
Behaviour	Based on trust.	Based on strength and fear.
Evaluation of acts	Constructive; supportive.	Suspicious; denigratory.
Settlement of conflicts	On basis of trust, adjustment and coordination.	On basis of fear and mistrust; solution imposed by stronger party.
Use of resources	Division of labour; efficient use of resources.	Duplication of work; waste of resources.
Pathogeny	Vested interests; nepotism; over-conformity; rigidity; (don't rock the boat); group-think.	Perceptual distortion; self-deception, the dialogue of the deaf; unwitting involvement towards escalation of conflict; coercion; mirror-imaging; stereotyping; simplistic thinking; mistrust.

Source: M. Deutsch, *The Resolution of Conflict*, Yale University Press, New Haven, 1973 (adapted)

respective goals. There will be division of labour but this will not be inflexibly held. Even between cooperating groups, conflicts will arise but these will be resolved on the basis of what is best for the joint task. Working in such cooperating groups is productive, both in terms of personal and group accomplishments. The more efficient use of the resources of men, money and materials can be measured by the greater productivity and the better outcome of their joint effort. The personal satisfaction of members in both groups will be evidenced through their lively and friendly relations which often spill over into outside joint activities.

The effects of competition run wholly in the opposite direction. Relations between the two groups are based on conflict, mistrust and fear. Both are competing for the same goal and each will do its utmost to wrest it from the other. There can only be one winner. There is no question of substituting for each other, each group welcoming the other's shortcomings and using them to reinforce their own advantage. The little communicating there will be will be misunderstood and perceived as hostile; information given by one group to the other will be automatically taken by the other as intended to mislead and will be decoded accordingly. The stronger group will use its greater power to dominate and impose its solution on the other. There is duplication of work, waste and therefore less productivity. Personal relations between the individuals in the two competing groups are practically non-existent and always unfriendly, negative and poor.

These findings have to be treated with discrimination. Each inter-group situation has to be studied in its particularities, for each such situation is unique at any one point in time, and specific to the groups involved. It is made up in the main of their past relationship and how they perceive their future goals and designs. Subject to this knowledge being had, most of the findings can be confirmed, through one's personal experience, in the home, at work, in industrial or international relations. They are valuable as means of understanding relations between groups, whether large or small. They illuminate the respective behaviours of the two small companies competing for the same order, as well as of the two superpowers competing for ideological supremacy; they explain the tremendous increase in productivity and solidarity that occur when competing groups lay down their differences and combine to face a common emergency, such as in wartime, for example.

Pathogeny in Groups

Both cooperation and competition are necessary to evolution and progress, when in healthy proportions and in appropriate combination. Even relations between competing groups are contained within a cooperative framework. Competing companies share an underlying sense of permissible limits and they have their rules of the game which are mutually accepted, even when not laid down in law. They play the game in the openness of the market. Competition here, within that framework, is invaluable in providing challenges, leading to finding the better alternative, the better product or service that satisfies more fully certain needs and wants. Two companies may be at each other's throats to gain the prize of an important order but their internecine war will be, generally, bounded by accepted standards of behaviour, by the rules of the game to which both adhere.

Cooperation and competition are, however, subject to disease. Competitiveness, as indeed cooperativeness, has a self-reinforcing character. Between competing groups, mistrust begets mistrust leading to higher levels of misperceptions, simplistic stereotyping and the dialogue of the deaf. The escalation towards greater conflict becomes inevitable; war is an example of pathological competitiveness. Conflicts of ideology and of religion, more or less the same thing, are the most virulent, invariably erupting in violence, and, these days, in terrorism. The lock-out and the strike are used by employers and workers respectively when they cannot resolve by other means their conflicting interests.

In the cooperating group, disease will take different forms. Perhaps, the most damaging to its health is over-conformity, always the result of group pressure. Experiments here, although of limited value because usually carried out under laboratory conditions, are indicative, nevertheless, of what happens in the open situation. One experiment consists in asking a number of people, say twelve, to note the number of items on the table, say ten. Eleven members of the group are told previously to give that number as nine. The twelfth, not privy to that knowledge, who says he saw ten retracts and changes it to nine, in the majority of cases, when asked again, after the others have replied. He is driven, without any overt compulsion, to deny the evidence of his own eyes and of his own counting. Overt pressure by the stronger party over the weaker members of the group is bad enough but, in principle at least, could be resisted. The covert coercion of the group, not consciously imposed by anyone in it, is much more insidious and therefore dangerous. It has to be recognized and guarded against.

The need for cohesiveness is misunderstood, when any expression of difference, be it of interest or of view, is taken as inimical to the well-being of the group as a whole. Uniformity will tend to make the group a closed system, a homogeneous mass of 'yes' people who do become nonentities, incapable or unwilling to assert themselves in any way, leading to general ineffectiveness and impoverishment, to the phenomenon of 'the group-think'.

Another degeneration in group health is the change in the character of the relations between its members. All members in the group are not of equal strength and the stronger ones may, or will, try to impose their views on the others. Differing interests, instead of being integrated into the overall group interest, become vested interests, each looking after the primacy of its own position. Cooperation moves along the continuum to the other end, to competition. The conflicts that arise between different departments, between directors, between management and work-force flow from these sections losing sight of their underlying interdependence and of their joint interest.

Nepotism is another kind of disease which can destroy a group. Managements which choose people because they are 'one of us' and will not rock the boat are not allowing new, different blood to revivify the group and keep it alive to the evolving realities. Autocratic unions, using the same 'one of us' method, offer a mirror-image of the tunnel-visioned managements and similarly reduce themselves and their members. Their respective nepotisms reinforce the division in the company and make it weak and ineffective – the kind of company that loses its market to its better-integrated competitors and very often is taken over by one of them.

The Cooperative Mutual Gains Strategy

Cooperation is not possible in all situations. Where aims clash, competition is inevitable, but it need not be all-exclusive. In business, it is certainly not always necessary to compete against a rival all along the line. It is possible to examine respective interests to find where it would mutually suit to cooperate and retain the competitive stance where it does not.

There is, of course, a great deal of cooperation going on all the time between clearly competing groups. Traders cooperate by operating in the same area, thus channelling greater customer-flow to all of them, and compete by offering different product and service packages. Professionals do the same by congregating in recognized places (the doctors in Harley Street, the lawyers in the Inns of Court) and competing through their different specialisms or, within the same specialism, through achieving difference in personal competence and reputation.

Relations between groups with conflicting interests, based on competition, will move to partial cooperation, as and when they begin to find an identity of interests. Companies used to guard all their trade information very jealously. As they learnt that each could derive valuable benefits if they shared some of it, they began to cooperate in this respect. Inter-firm comparisons of costs, profit margins, stock-turn rates, returns on capital and other similar financial criteria are now used, as a matter of course, by companies to relate and assess their performance against those in the same line of business.

Research is now very expensive and many organizations, from computer companies to car manufacturers, are collaborating in research work to share costs. The participants in the research projects, all direct competitors, could not carry out the research on their own, because of the high level of investment required and the need for 'critical mass' brainpower to get it off the ground. They get their specialists to work together in a neutral location to tackle ideas at the pre-competitive stage, when so little research has been done that no one can tell for sure that it will become a commercial proposition or, if it does, whether it will benefit one more than the others.

Something even more specific than this goes on in advertising, where the holder of the biggest market share will advertise to increase total demand for the generic product. He knows that his competitors, who will have contributed nothing to the cost, will derive some benefit from the campaign, but he reckons that he will get at least, and likely more than, his relative share of the extra demand he will have generated. In a market where demand is still low or has reached a stagnant low plateau, his better advantage lies in lifting total demand to a higher level, not in trying to attract his competitors' customers.

Manufacturers and retailers used to think their interests diverged and used to fight their own corner against each other. As they came to understand their interdependence better and realized that working together would better meet their individual interests, they changed their relationship into a cooperative one. The large retailer who previously screwed his suppliers for the last penny now understands that this does not pay. If he does not help his suppliers to make a decent profit, they may go out of business, leaving him high and dry or, if there are shortages or delays, they are unlikely to give him preferential treatment.

The fast-moving computer industry provides an example where failure to cooperate has worked to its detriment and also to that of existing and potential users. Most manufacturers preferred to tie customers to their proprietary operating systems to stop them buying equipment from competitors. They had to give way, one by one, but, even by 1990, the agreed standards which would allow users to plug pieces of equipment from different makers into the one system were still not fully in place. This made it more difficult to meet the needs of customers for 'open systems', the straightforward networks that can provide simple connections between large and small computers. Through their myopic vision of competing all along the line, initiated and kept up for a long time by the leader in the industry, they missed seeing their best joint interest and succeeded in reducing potential demand for their wares, to their individual loss.

Not every business yet realizes the full extent of the added values to be derived from cooperating in areas of mutual interest. New organizational forms will evolve when the benefits of partial cooperation are better understood. Inevitably, companies will have to move in that direction, as the escalating costs of ever more sophisticated technology and the need for greater brainpower make themselves felt. The signs are already apparent in the increasing use of joint ventures, in sub-contracting and licensing arrangements, in franchising. The partial alliances being formed between competing companies to tackle the single European market are yet another example of the evolving cooperative mutual-gains strategy. Success will go to those business leaders who have the vision to go for this newer strategy and the ingenuity to devise the ways and means of implementing it, in the use of resources or the development and creation of markets.

Dynamics of Group Relations

That the effects of cooperation are superior, on the whole, to those of competition is not a new discovery. Cooperating groups have formed from time immemorial to derive the benefits of cooperation. What is perhaps not sufficiently understood is the dynamic of the relations and their self-fulfilling character.

The perception one has of the other party colours one's attitude and determines one's behaviour. If you think that B is a moron, you treat him like one; this induces him to respond in that way, which confirms you in your opinion and reinforces your subsequent behaviour towards him; at the end of the day, you are convinced that he is effectively stupid. Another person who thinks B reasonably intelligent treats him as such; he gets in return intelligent reactions which confirm his original opinion of B and which lead him to continue treating B as sensible; at the end of the day, he is convinced the individual is quite bright.

Attitudes in cooperative or competitive situations affect perceptions of the other groups and are similarly self-fulfilling in their results. We saw earlier that, in the cooperating groups, they regarded each other as friendly and helpful which made them behave towards each other in openness and trust, whereas, in the competing groups, mistrust between them bred more mistrust and more hostility.

The party who is open and trusting will evoke a similar reciprocal response from the other, and the relationship, strengthened by continuous displays of good faith, will come to rest on trust – a cooperative situation. On the other hand, members of competing groups mistrust each other and, through the process of mounting reciprocity, the relationship becomes embedded in mistrust – a competitive situation. Many management–workforce relations have, because of their past history, become deeply set in mistrust and all its negative ramifications.

It is difficult to move from the competitive to the cooperative mode, from mistrust to trust. If one party decides it is better for itself to stop competing and to start cooperating, it must create the new climate by initiating itself the change in the relationship. It will now behave in an open and truthful manner, but cannot expect immediate similar reciprocity. One trusting action will not automatically erase their past relationship. It takes time to change perceptions. The first party will have to persevere, by continuous displays of trust. Suspicion lurks in the background, the strength of which depends upon how mistrustful their relationship had previously been. Any one of its actions, even though friendly but misconstrued by the other as hostile, will make the relationship which had been evolving towards cooperativeness, backslide into mistrust and competitiveness.

It takes time to build trust between two groups previously competing against each other. The changing relationship between the USSR and the USA is a fascinating illustration of the ebbs and flows of replacing mistrust with trust. Reagan's formula of 'trust and verify' showed the psychological inability of the USA to accept at face value the Soviet overtures and Gorbachev had to continue his displays of good faith. Still, the evolving, trusting relationship remains fragile. The past retains its hold and can only be changed through continuously different experience, spread over time.

Understanding the dynamics of group relations is essential to the modern manager. Managers, at whatever level they may be, who trust and share their knowledge with their people will, in return, learn much from them. Sharing knowledge and experience creates the group where each wants to give of his best. The work, as a result, is done to a high standard and on time. Managers who hold their cards close to their chest and play one individual against another, will evoke similar responses from them. They create the confused and insecure group where each, not knowing how he stands, follows the leader's example and goes his own way. Division, conflict and poor work follow. Managers here will blame those in their group for lack of cooperation and perhaps never realize that it is mostly due to their own doing.

Groundwork for Effective Group-work

This summary of group formation, relations and dynamics indicates some of the prerequisites for successful group-working on a continuing basis. They include:

1 *The manager as an integral part of his group.*

Managers should never forget that they are the head of their team, whether this be the section, the department, the division or the whole company; but, equally, they should never forget that they are an integral part of it, always in and of their group. It is essential to absorb this concept of integrality of all in the group. It does not come easily, for its opposite, that of separatedness, is deeply anchored in our Western culture. Managers cannot do truly good work, fulfil their function of effectively organizing the task of their groups, unless they themselves connect with their members on the basis of reciprocation. Shades of the past, of the 'I am the boss; you do as I say' type have to be resisted. Managers, and none more so than directors, should watch themselves: when their thinking and acting is backing into the obsolete past, they must bring themselves firmly into the present.

2 *Using the whole man.*

Individuals are composite beings, woven of many parts. They bring to the work-place the totality of themselves, the same set of characteristics, albeit differently projected, that actuate them at home and elsewhere. They cannot dichotomize themselves, even if they

want to, taking to work their rational selves and leaving the
supposedly irrational half – instincts, feelings, emotions, prejudices –
at home. The 'economic' person is now at last seen to be an
abstraction. So should all the other attempts be to isolate a particular
characteristic and use it as the description of the whole person. There
is the individual as the rat; as the spiritual being; as the thinking
animal; as the political animal; and so on – as many varieties as
Heinz's. No individual is any one of these alone, but all of them
together, with different weightings, of course, and probably one or
more dominant characteristics, but each influencing the others and
being influenced in its turn. Feelings and prejudices are facts, just as
'hard' as those that can be measured; that they are not so easily
quantifiable does not invalidate their relevance, does not make them
any less real; ignoring them does not make them go away.

Managers have to identify as many of these characteristics as
possible in the individual and address themselves to the 'whole' man
and to 'whole' men together. Effective managing, the sort that will
release and use people's full energies, appeals to something more
than a bit of the person. If the hard head is accompanied by a soft
heart, it is a waste not to use both.

3 *Establishing the group objectives.*

People join an employing company as individuals for a variety of
personal reasons, each with his own objectives and aspirations. They
have to be integrated into the work-team that knows its tasks and the
reasons behind them. It devolves upon the chief executive, as the
overall head of the group, to articulate the corporate aims. The need
to communicate changed goals is obvious; that to keep them known,
even when unchanged, is also imperative. It falls to managers to do
the same specifically for their group, always relating the group-task to
the wider objectives of the company.

It is not only the 'how' but also the 'why' of the task that must be
shared with all those involved in it. Full commitment cannot be had,
unless everyone in the group knows the whys and has taken a part,
however small, in the decision-making process that went to make up
the objective. Participation by the workers in the decision-making
process is, in fact, a basic necessity, in recognition of the simple
psychological truth that involvement means involvement. People
simply cannot commit themselves wholeheartedly to aims they do not
share and have not taken a part in developing. Shrewdness is as

prevalent amongst workers as it is amongst directors and the workers can acquire the kind of general knowledge required at board level to back their experience. Having worker-representatives on boards of directors is not, as some would have it, socialism. To hold such a view is to be actuated by misguided and obsolete ideology, set in the past when management and work-force saw each other as adversaries; it is not looking forward to building the future upon the newer understanding of integrating needs and interests.

Influence is always reciprocal. Imposed direction is reciprocated by sullen and unwilling acceptance, the acceptance that will stick to the rule-book and hang the consequences. All managers, whatever their position in the hierarchy, must remain open to being influenced, if they want to influence. Otherwise, they revert to the old outmoded command–obedience syndrome, or their influencing becomes simply manipulating techniques, neither of which works well in the modern world.

4 *Exchanging fair values.*

The 'what's in it for me' principle, inherent in all cooperative work, has to be assessed. Contributions have to be matched with appropriate rewards. The higher up managers are, the greater is their responsibility to create wealth and to grasp the importance of its 'fair' distribution as a means of realizing it. What is 'fair' is a very large question indeed and changes over time, depending upon a multitude of factors. One of these is the view taken of the actual contributions made: if seen as unimportant, their low reward will be considered just and fair; they will be valued and rewarded more highly, if seen as valuable and indispensable to the whole.

The differentials in the reward packages between the various contributing groups will be more readily accepted, if considered to be fair. Managers who feather-bed themselves by way of very high compensation packages do not, as is usually held, evoke envy in all. They evoke a sense of injustice and unfairness which bounces back against them in reduced cooperation. There are already rumblings in the UK that some managements are overstepping the bounds of propriety in the compensation packages they award themselves. Appeals to wage restraint would be more successful if directors, by example, led the way.

The monetary reward is but one side of self-interest. Self-interest is many-sided. It includes money of course, but also self-esteem, the satisfaction of knowing that one's contribution has been essential to the whole and that it is valued; it includes the enjoyment and the satisfaction derived from solving problems with others and getting a job well done; the solidarity and the sense of belongingness developed from striving to make the better product, to provide the better service that will attach the customer to the firm and detach him from its competitors. Some managers may not be wholly responsible for the monetary rewards of the people in their team but the non-monetary rewards are exclusively within the province of every manager: he creates the right work-environment where these intangibles can develop and grow and of course this redounds to the greater benefit, material and otherwise, of all.

5 *Welcoming difference.*

Heraclitus said: 'Nature desires eagerly opposites and, out of them, it completes its harmony, not out of similars.' Managers would do well to ponder upon this.

It was seen earlier that one of the dangers to the continued well-being of the group is that of over-conformity, of every one in it becoming the same, leading to the group-think, the sheep mentality which augurs its death. Wishy-washy harmony is not the thing to be considered; it leads nowhere. However outlandish a person's views may be, they will contain grains of truth embedded in his logic and prejudices. It is much more fruitful, much more productive to bring the differences into the open, to extract these grains of truth and use them. It is in this way that managers will build their team into the group that grows and develops, making each one a full participant in the action.

6 *Connecting, always connecting.*

The job of managers is not done unless they connect their group effectively with the others in the company. This is still merely part of their job. The company is itself part of the bigger grouping comprising its shareholders, bankers, suppliers, customers and general public and needs their goodwill and loyalty. To get these, managers have to deal with them honestly and openly, sharing with them, as far as possible, objectives and aspirations. Managements very often justify not spending money on pollution control by thinking that shareholders won't stand for it. How do they know actually? Perhaps, they would. They could at least ask them.

Managers should not only themselves connect, but also get

members of their teams to connect. Those who send their people to work in other departments of the company, to trade exhibitions, or to the customers' own factories are enabling them to develop the wider perspective of understanding how their own small part fits into the bigger whole; from such openings flow a greater interest in the job and the initiatives and ideas which result in specific improvements.

E. M. Forster said it all when he ended his *Passage to India* with the memorable phrase: 'Connect, only connect.'

These guidelines are not easy to put into practice; some are more difficult than others. Relations are not always right. They may have started or may have degenerated and become fixed into adversarial positions in which individuals or groups of individuals oppose each other, leading to the wasteful effects of unnecessary competition. Work-places are more like adversarial, political arenas, rather too often.

Esprit de corps can however be regenerated and built up. The history of management is full of examples of great managers who have turned their company, their department, or their section, into exciting places of work and secured effective performance from the group, even in the most unpromising physical conditions. A first-class manager will always strive to emulate the great exemplars; and, by so doing, become himself an exemplar.

Effective managing, discussed in the next chapter, provides the key to building that team spirit on which so much depends.

Notes

1 Mary Parker Follett, *The New State*, Longmans, Green, London, 1920, p. 21.
2 Muzarif Sherif, *Group Conflict and Cooperation*, Routledge & Kegan Paul, London, 1949.

3

The Managing Process:
Relating, Coordinating,
Controlling

The accepted formula for successful management is given as 'knowledge–experience–communication'. Most managers nowadays start with a degree or professional qualification and/or some business training and go on to acquire the relevant experience in the field. Good companies will provide additional learning facilities to update the knowledge. On the whole, there seems to be little difficulty about the 'knowledge' leg of the management tripod. 'Experience' can be a little more difficult, but is gained by managers being moved between the different departments or divisions within the company, or their moving between companies, between industries and between countries. Neither 'knowledge' nor 'experience' seems to be a stumbling block.

'Communication', however, is in a rather different category. How to use machines, materials and money was taught in depth, but not how to use the much more complex resource of human beings. It is only relatively recently that it has come into its own as a core skill that managers have to learn and acquire. This late recognition of 'communication' as an essential ingredient of management has led to the growth of a real industry in it; it is now taught as a subject in all professional and management studies and on its own in specific courses of varying duration. Yet, despite the considerable attention given to it, managers seem to fail to acquire the magic skill. When managers are asked what is their most pressing need, communicating invariably tops their list. It is worthwhile investigating the reasons for the difficulty before discussing the managing process proper.

A Historical Digression

Perhaps the fundamental reason for the difficulty is that communicating is still seen essentially as a one-way affair, flowing from managers to their subordinates. A shorthand, current definition of management, found in most textbooks, is that 'managers get things done *through* their people'. Communicating, in this context, is thus seen as how best they can get their views and directions *through* to their subordinates. The more forward-looking managers will explain, to varying degree, the whys and wherefores and will look for feedback to monitor the extent to which they have been understood and followed. However, the underlying premise generally remains that they are in a different category from them: managers command and subordinates obey.

Directors, for example, do not see themselves as being in the same category as the workers; they themselves are not perceived as 'workers' by the workforce. There is 'the management' and there are 'the workers'. Here and there, a director will proclaim 'We are all workers now', a novelty which confirms the newness of the concept. The same sense of being separate and superior to the lower level in the hierarchy informs all echelons in the organization. It is not so long ago that status differences between white- and blue-collared workers were abolished. The form of reward still remains different: workers are paid overtime for the extra hours they work; managers would not like to be so compensated. The feeling of superior separatedness lingers on.

This sense of superior separatedness can be traced back to the Cartesian notion of '*Cogito ergo sum*', the axiomatic 'I think therefore I am' taught to every child. Descartes was one of the thinkers in the sixteenth century who ushered in the scientific revolution. He also bequeathed to us the artificial and wrong mind–body dichotomy, still embedded in Western culture: thinking is separate from doing, and is superior to it. From this follows, albeit at many removes, the doctrine that managers are the brains and the managed the brawn.

More directly, the view of the managing, organizing function was inherited from the state, the church and military systems, where the head was considered separate from the others, the fount of all knowledge and the sole arbiter of action. A command, issued as an order, was carried through the obedience, enforced if necessary, of subordinates. The development of the railways, in the third quarter of the nineteenth century in the USA, had required the creation of whole new organizations from scratch. Business had no model to copy, except the large-scale organization of the army. The railway companies in the USA were thus structured basically on the command/obedience principles of the army. The large industrial businesses which followed were organized on a similar pattern. Much of the vocabulary of management for the next seventy years came from analogies from the army. In the UK, because of its size and the ad hoc way in which the railways were built, the need for the large-scale organization did not arise until the 1920s.

Then, 'scientific management' introduced by Frederick W. Taylor and his disciples in the early part of this century reinforced the status quo, by offering a 'scientific' basis for the separation between thinking and doing and for the strict command/obedience communication system. Taylor argued for 'the one best way', the 'scientific' search for the 'objective standard' for any piece of work, done by 'a first-class' man in favourable conditions. It was the duty of management to determine correct methods of work by careful analysis; to provide suitable machinery and good working conditions; and to select those who would be 'first-class' at the job. Once the 'scientific' production had been worked out by management, workers would be trained to do exactly what they were told and would then be expected to obey in a docile manner. No initiative whatsoever was permissible and any derogation from the strict application of the method taught was to be punished by fines and in the last resort by firing. The workers were the hands, 'paid to work and not to think'.

'Scientific management' or 'Taylorism' as it also was known generated much controversy in the USA, both from workers and employers. Gompers, one of the then frontline American trade union leaders, described it quite accurately:

Here is the idea that all labour consists simply in moving things. See? Just as all the work done by the machines is one motion after another, all manipulation of matter by human beings is made up of motions and series of motions. So there you are, wage earners, in general, were machines – considered industrially of course.[1]

The employers did not like it much either, as 'objective standards' circumscribed their authority and power. They did not like either the 'mental revolution' Taylor was advocating to go alongside his 'scientific management'. Most of them simply used the relevant bits to keep workers in their place, and as a lever to pay them less for more work. Gilbreth, one of the leaders in the scientific management movement and the foremost seeker of the 'one best way', realizing how it could be used against the workers and that the 'mental revolution' was a long way off, would refuse any assignment from any employer whom he suspected would use it unfairly.

Interestingly enough, the Japanese lapped it up. Taylor's *Principles of Scientific Management*, published in 1911, came just at the right time for Japan, when the government and the *zaibatsus*, their large trading companies, were anxious to bring themselves up to Western industrial standards. Japan, then, was sending large missions of technicians and businessmen to the USA and to Europe under their *wakon konsai* (Japanese spirit, Western techniques) slogan. A Japanese engineer, in the USA at the time, ignoring the 'scientific' claim of Taylor's principles wrote, in the same year, his own interpretation in a book which he entitled *Secrets for Eliminating Futile Work and Increasing Production*. This brought the virtues of the new methods to the general Japanese public. His book sold one million copies in ten years – an amazing quantity for the period. *Mitsubishi* distributed two hundred thousand copies to his employees and another *zaibatsu* president fifty thousand to his. In early 1913, Taylor's own book was translated into Japanese.

In France, Taylorism was studied and spread by top engineers and chemists who combined it with what Fayol, at around the same time, was teaching about general and industrial administration. It spread through the rest of the Continent but was strongly resisted in the UK, with its well-established trade union movement and the Quaker background of many of the country's employers.

In the main, 'scientific management' took hold in different guises and became the method of organization in industrial production. Motion and work study, in its variants, was still prevalent in the late 1960s. There was opposition to the movement in its own time. There have been, since then, a bewildering array of new schools of management thought: the human relationists, the managerial stylists, the organizational theorists, to name but a few. However, the underlying philosophy of Taylorism continued to prevail. It still prevails, under other names. It has entered for example into the provision of services, now run on industrial lines. Some fast-food chains issue detailed and exact instructions of the steps its employees, whether cooking or serving, have to follow, in order to achieve uniform and set standards. In general, the modern view, however, is to seek 'the better way' and it is no longer held that management alone is capable of finding it.

We no longer see the manager as all-supreme. We have moved on – to the hands-on manager, to managing by wandering about, to the new concept that 'we are all workers now', all these notions evolving to close that gap between management and workers. But centuries of conditioning cannot be undone in a few decades. Intellectual understanding is one thing and habit another. It takes time to change habits of thought and behaviour bred in the mind and the bone. The command/obedience sequence still permeates underlying attitudes.

To add to the psychological difficulty and because of it, communicating itself is not yet thoroughly understood. Being a relatively new subject of study, there is still confusion as to its nature. Some equate it with interacting; others hold that interaction is more basic than communication and comes first; generally the subject is taught in a superficial way, mostly as techniques the manager should acquire to influence others, whether superiors, peers or subordinates. Techniques are certainly useful as they save time but not, as in this case, when they are based on outmoded ideas. What has happened is that the straightforward, direct command being no longer acceptable, resort is being made to its assumed alternative: influencing. But influencing is, at the end of the day, still the old command/obedience garb, inadequately altered to suit the new need. All in all, it is no wonder that managers find it difficult to acquire the kind of communicating skill that will mobilize the potential of the combined knowledge and experience of their teams. First and foremost, they need to understand the managing process, for communicating is of its essence.

The Managing Process

The managing process is older than man and universal. Its universality springs from the framework of relations from which life itself emerges and develops. Specialization and division of work and its combination and integration are found in every living organism.

Follett recognized the managing process as the organizing activity that goes on in the plant, animal, individual, the group whether small or large. The process relates, coordinates and controls the contributions of the various sub-systems, integrating them into the functional and functioning unit, as it adjusts to its environment, in reciprocal interaction with it. Self-managing is the basis of life. It goes on unconsciously in the plant and animal and, at varying levels of consciousness, in man. It is, for example, in the individual, the process, both conscious and unconscious, of relating, coordinating and controlling his movements as he gets out of bed in the morning. The purpose of the ongoing activity is to enable the organism to survive and prosper. Since the distinguishing mark of human nature is its capacity for reasoning, it has learnt on the whole how to improve the managing process. In some cases, however, it has also succeeded in distorting it. The better we understand the managing process and correctly carry it out, the more effectively we can integrate with our milieu.

The managing system is already in place in the individual at birth. The intricate connections between his limbs and organs hold him together as a unit. The baby has to learn that, physically, it is a separate entity from its environment and to learn how best to relate with it.

In the group, made up of separate physical individuals, the managing system has to be created and put in place to enable its members properly to connect with each other. This is, for example, what the Highway Code does for the members of the driving public. It formalizes the process through which they relate, coordinate and control their actions when driving, for effectiveness and safety, and also regulates their reciprocal relations with pedestrians at the same time and to the same end. Drivers and pedestrians manage each other through the Highway Code and through the system of lights and other physical signs created better to facilitate the process.

In the organized and permanent group, the process has also to be codified into a system and, in addition, has to be mediated through specific appointees to carry it out. Professional management comes into its own. Managers carry out the process of relating, coordinating and controlling the work of the members of their groups so as to fulfil the given task. Job specifications, work manuals, rule-books, organization charts and so on codify the rules and procedures of the managing system. Even in the large group, the managing process does not have to be mediated exclusively through individuals. Just as in traffic movement, the lights system has replaced traffic police, so, in the organization, the new technology has replaced managers at many intermediate levels. The process itself remains, however, essential.

An important point about the process is that its components – relating, coordinating, controlling – are not sequential steps but different aspects of it in dynamic interaction. The process is indivisible. Where there is effective relating, there is *ipso facto* proper coordinating and controlling. These elements will be considered separately but this is solely to facilitate analysis, not to suggest degrees of importance or significance. Each is part of the others and, together, they form the process as a whole. Follett was adamant that it is not possible to relate first, then coordinate and finally control. The elements interlock and overlap in any order and in any proportion.

The sales manager who sits down to agree the sales estimate with one of his salespeople is relating with him in discussing the estimate; the manager is also controlling him for, as a result of agreement, the salesperson is expected to produce the sales as estimated. The process is reciprocal, for the manager is also influenced within certain parameters by the salesperson. If the salesperson convinces him that he can do better than, or not as well as, the estimate on the table, the manager will have been influenced, that is, controlled, by the salesperson to the extent that he increases or decreases the estimate.

When the time comes to control the performance, say after a month, the manager will still be relating with the salesperson: relating actual sales and profits against estimate, analysing the reasons for the variances against plan and deciding, on the basis of the outcome as it has turned to be, future action. Again, the relating will be reciprocal, for the salesperson will bring to the meeting his knowledge and experience of the field: better sales than estimated because he has been able to sign on a large customer, or because customers have found a new use for the product, or because a competitor is losing his grip; conversely, lower sales than estimated, because another product has come on the market, or the competitor is hotting up on advertising, or delivery dates are better.

Any one of these reasons will lead to a different decision being taken by the manager, a decision that would not have been possible without the salesperson's input. A declining competitor, a new use for the product open up different growth opportunities for the company; greater competition, whether by way of a new product on the market, or better advertising or delivery dates, represents a threat which perhaps has to be nipped in the bud or kept on hold for later action.

In this scenario, the manager, in the process of controlling the salesperson, is, in fact, being controlled by him, if the manager takes any action flowing from the salesperson's informational input. The salesperson will not only have influenced his own direct manager but, through him, the other managers in the company: those who will be induced to look at the company's own advertising (to promote the new use of the product likely to bring the company a completely new customer-segment, or to improve it to counteract the competitors); or those in production (to give quicker deliveries); or those in research (to study the new product on the market).

The scenario could have unfolded differently. It may be that the sales are below estimate because the salesperson did not call on as many customers as he should have done and is using the competitor's advertising as an excuse to hide his own shortcomings. In the good work-situation, where relationships are based on openness and trust, the salesperson would admit he missed some important calls and explain why. However, things may not be as they should, or could, be. The manager cannot take the salesperson's reason at face value. He has to be convinced of its validity. The manager already would have seen the new advertising campaign and made his own assessment of its likely impact. He will ask himself and the salesperson many questions. How have the other salespeople, subject to that same condition, fared? What's the past performance of this salesperson like? On how many customers did he call? Which ones? Why not the others? Is there some difficulty in the home? Is the travelling schedule right, or is he wasting too much time on the road? Is he getting the right back-up services? Is he just becoming bored? If yes, does he need a new challenge? Or is he just becoming lazy, in need of a pep talk?

Even if the manager has no cause to doubt the veracity of the salesperson, he still has to assess the reasons given, to disentangle the relevant from the irrelevant and focus on the relevant factor which needs action. In any one scenario or situation, the managing process is always the same: relating, coordinating, controlling facts, figures, perceptions from the relevant surrounding complex, in order to take effective action relative to the task in hand.

Relating

Relating, one of the strands of the managing process, is based on information and the interpretation of that information. What information individuals select and how they use it depends on a complex of factors: their attitudes, both general and specific to the matter in hand; the store of information they already have; and their need and purpose.

The sales manager who is told by the salesperson that his sales are below estimate because of the competitor's more aggressive advertising will, in assessing the validity of the salesperson's conclusion, be affected by his attitude towards him. He will tend to take it seriously, if he knows the salesperson is shrewd and hard-working; he will tend to dismiss it, if he thinks the salesperson unreliable and slapdash. If, however, he himself has seen the advertisements and rated them highly, and the other salespeople have also failed their sales estimates, he will attach more credence to the salesperson's assertion, even if he does not rate him highly. The action taken will again depend on the store of information he possesses. If he knows that the company is releasing a new advertising campaign the following week, he will wait to see its effects on sales; otherwise, others will be alerted to the threat which has appeared in order to take corrective action.

Out of the same apparently objective situation, two individuals with very much the same knowledge but with different purposes will select different facts or, if they choose the same facts, will combine them differently to come to different interpretations. The employer and the trade union representative select different facts to interpret the one particular fact – the employer's offer on the table – differently. The employer chooses those facts which show it as generous and straining their resources to meet it; the workers' representative those which show it as too close and well below the employer's paying capacity. Two experts, both eminent in the same field, one acting for the defence and the other for the prosecution, will, on the same facts of the case, arrive at diametrically opposed submissions.

In the work-situation where the relations are not adversarial and the purpose is to get the job well done, appropriate action will flow from effective relatings. Each party knows something about the job that the others do not: the manager about task-totality and task connections, the workers about their actual capacity and the intricacies of their job. Each day brings new events which require rearranging the situation in some particular. It is out of these informational inputs, to which everyone contributes, and out of the consequent changing pool of information, that underlying existing facts surface. These can then be linked to the known ones, and new and better interlinkings formed. As a result, the job gets done better as a whole. Follett always maintained that effective relating evokes and creates.

Relating, communicating, interacting are very much words of the same ilk. To attempt to deduce what comes first as, for example, whether interacting is antecedent to communicating is futile and mere semantic quibbling. Communicating is not limited to verbal or written exchanges but includes all that goes on between two or more parties, as they interact, as they manage their relations.

There is always a strong tendency to think in linear terms, in terms of cause and effect. This is very much in evidence when the communicating process (which is the same as the relating or interacting process) is explained. There is, to begin with, the sender of a message and then a recipient who responds to it, this response then returning to the sender as feedback and influencing them in any subsequent message. There is a stimulus which is the cause, and a response which is the effect. This is a mechanistic view of the process which, discretely separating stimulus from response or cause from effect, does not reflect accurately what happens in reality. When we come to analyse any happening, we invariably find that cause and effect are so inextricably mixed that it is impossible to disentangle them from each other. They are part of each other in reciprocal interaction.

Follett studied the process carefully and saw it in its dynamic complexity. She held that stimulus is not cause and response effect but that, together, they form an interlocking, self-sufficing process. Response is not merely the activity resulting from a certain stimulus and that response in turn influencing the activity. It is *because* it is response that it influences it. As she put it:

We shall never catch the stimulus stimulating or the response responding . . . My response is not to a crystallized product of the past, static for the moment of meeting; *while* I am behaving, the environment is changing because of my behaving and my behaviour is a response to the new situation which I, in part, have created . . . the responding is not merely to another activity, but to the relating between the self-activity and the other activity.[2]

If this makes your head reel a bit, you are in good company. Follett recounts that a professor of philosophy told her it made him dizzy to talk with her because 'he wished always to compare varying things with something stationary'.

There is however nothing stationary in life. All is in perpetual becoming, however imperceptibly change may be taking place. The process may be difficult to conceptualize because of our mechanistic ways of looking at things but it goes on all the time. Follett called it 'circular response'.

Take a game of tennis, for example. A serves. The way A serves will depend in part on how he expects B to respond. In serving, in providing the initial stimulus, A has already, in fact, responded to B's feedback, not to the actual feedback, but to his imagined feedback, the way he expects B will respond. The way B returns the ball depends partly upon the way it is served. A's next play will depend on the original serve plus the return of B and so on. The same interaction goes on in a game of chess. Each player, in making any one move, is anticipating his opponent's likely responses two, three or more moves ahead. Or you find that C stimulates you. You become more intelligent, or more generous, or more active when you are with him. This is because there is something in C which brings out these characteristics in you. There is good chemistry between you and C. In every case, the reaction is not only to the other party but also to the relation which exists between the two parties.

In human relations, I never react to you but to you+me. It is I+you reacting to you+me. I can never influence *you* because *you* have already influenced me. Response is always to a relating, the relation between 'the response and that to which the response is being made'. It is that relation, that activity going on between the parties that determines their behaviour. When a business is finding out as much as it can about its competitors, it knows that they are also doing the same and it has to act, not only in relation to the existing situation, but also to that it thinks is likely to evolve, from its knowledge, actual or assumed, of what the competitors are likely to be doing.

The 'circular response' process is basic in physiology. Follett held that it was the basic truth in all the social sciences. Very slowly, this understanding is seeping through. Figure 3.1 indicates the two ways of seeing the relating or communicating process.

The Field of Control

Before going on with the other two strands of the managing process, it is useful to look at the field of control – the area of activity the individual can affect and, therefore, to that extent, control. Whilst, in

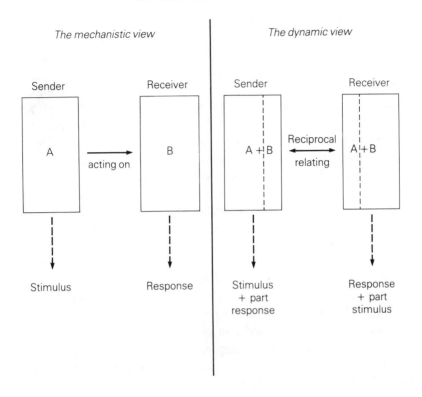

Figure 3.1   The communicating or relating process

any activity, the managing process is always the same, the field of control is not. This radiates from the activity itself and is relative to it.

The recognized field of control of the salesperson is his sales area. The way he controls it depends upon how he relates with existing and potential customers and also with those people at the centre on whom the salesperson depends to satisfy these customers. The field of control of the sales manager is different and bigger. He does not have the same close contact with the customers and the market that his salespeople have, but he is responsible for all their activities and much else besides.

As managers move up to bigger responsibilities, their fields of control become different, losing in specificity of detail and gaining in more activities to direct. Their fields of control become wider and more complex to operate. It requires as a result the wider outlook and the better vision. Chief executives have the largest complex to control and need, amongst other things, the largest and most discriminating vision to encompass the much broader and fluid environment in which their company operates and which they have to influence.

Fields of control cannot be held in separate watertight compartments. At their extremities, they spill over their neighbours with which they interact. Salesperson A may not look after his area well and one of his customers is not happy with his service. That customer will be meeting business friends and may be asked by one of them for a view as to whether to use that company. His answer will not be favourable. Salesperson B, covering the area serving that potential customer, will not gain this particular business, and the company will therefore lose it. Salesperson A has controlled B's performance and that of the company in that particular respect, even though the activity was outside his own field.

Managers need to know how far the contribution of any one member of their group affects the overall task. The job specification, the organization chart can never reflect the actual field of control of any one participant; detailed and exact as they may be, they cannot replicate reality. Take, for example, the telephonist. He comes well down the organization chart but his field of control is very wide. He is the link controlling *inter alia* part of the company's external relations and his action – say failure to pass on a customer's call – may lose the company the important order it had been working on for months.

Managers have to see the situation as a whole and how individual tasks interlink to make that whole. And, of course, they have to make the part/whole relationship of any job clear to its holder. If the telephonist were shown his strategic spot in the company's scheme of things, he would be aware of his value and relevance to the company, be more conscious of his responsibility and more likely to fulfil it better.

Coordinating

Coordinating, the second strand of the managing process, is effective relating. DIY assemblers know that, in whatever object they are putting together, it is essential to co-relate its components in their interlocking connections. You may bring together the parts of a machine, but you cannot have an operating machine until you have fitted them each with the other in their relational order. As with the object or machine, so with any activity, whatever it may be: for it to be performed satisfactorily, its elements must be integrated in their orderly functional relatings. The more complex the activity or set of activities, the greater the need to organize the subsumed parts in coherent interaction.

Coordinating is the crux of almost everything managers have to do. They need to identify the various elements in the separate activities of their unit, understand the reciprocal dependencies and connect them in their proper relations to bring about the successful performance of the task as a whole; and also and concurrently, managers must fit the activities of their unit with those of the others in the business, to ensure the overall attainment of its objectives.

An example from the retail trade rather than from a complex manufacturing industry will best serve to illustrate the process. The scenario: a new selling department manager who wants to achieve higher turnover at more profit, with no increase in costs and with existing resources of staff, merchandise and supporting services. The manager sets about this by creating his field of control and extracting from his environmental complex, as they are able to envision it, those facts relevant to the purpose. The manager asks:

1 *Who are my customers?*
   Are they young, old, staid, lively? Are they married or single and, if both, in what likely proportions? What ethnic groups do they belong to and, if mixed, in what proportions of blacks, coloureds, whites? Are they all well-off, poor or a mixture of both? And so on.

2 *Who may they be?*
   Perhaps I could increase my customers; will the local and national papers help to identify new customer segments? Can my colleagues tell me about local events, tourist influx, school holidays? What would be the most appropriate merchandise for these potential customer-groups? When are they likely to come in?

3 *What about my department?*
   Is it well laid-out for ease of customer-flow? Will it make it easier if I move this fixture from here to there? Relative to the customers expected this week, what merchandise should I bring forward?

4 *What about the merchandise?*
   Does it meet the needs of our customers, in terms of function, price, design? What are we selling best? What is it about that item

which is appealing to our customers? We sold 50 of it at £9.99 in my first morning at work. Why?

5 *What about the staff?*

Are their hours of work best organized to fit well with our pattern of trade? When are we busiest? What are the regulations regarding National Insurance contributions for part-time workers? A has children to look after and needs to leave early; how can I fit that in? C's sales are very high. How does he do it? Perhaps I could get C to take the half-hour training session next week?

6 *What about my competitors?*

Who are they, exactly? What are they offering relative to us? Is some of their merchandise better than ours? If so, in what ways: price, design, function? What is their shopping ambience like? Their level of service? Their fixtures? What can I learn from them?

Each new fact the manager acquires leads him to new insights, to more questions. He builds his own picture and situation, fitting in the various factors relative to each other, and deciding how to adjust these factors better among themselves. The same actuality was there to be had by his predecessor but the new manager sees and organizes it differently. How long it takes him to create his own picture depends upon the facts of the particular case: whether he has been promoted from the same branch, from another branch or is totally new to the company; whether he is new to, or familiar with, the merchandise he is now selling. The manager has to be careful not to act hastily and on isolated facts but, already, if he has some experience, he is likely to:

1 *At the end of the first day:* link with the central buyer. 'We have sold 50 of item X; the customers are . . . ; they are buying it because . . . ; I have only got 25 left; I think it will be a good seller at least for the coming month; I think we could sell here about 400 a week; could I have 200 for Saturday trading? I'll ring you on Monday morning to let you know how they have sold.'

2 *At the end of the third day:* discuss the point with the staff and together move that fixture from here to there.

3 *At the end of the fifth day:* rearrange, with the staff, the positioning of merchandise and fixtures of the department, to prepare it for Saturday trading and to promote item X, received that morning.

4 *At the end of the first week:* find that his actual turnover is 10 per cent above estimate as against 4 per cent above estimate for the same

department in the other branches of the chain. Moving that fixture did help the customers to get more easily to the merchandise and to buy; item X sold out.

At the end of his first week, the manager has influenced all those included in his field of control: the customers who, by word of mouth, will be relaying to their friends about item X and that it is easier now to shop in that department; the central buyer who will be reacting to the manager's performance and registering that he is a go-getter and knows his stuff; the general manager who will be pleased with the result and will be more amenable, if he continues to do well, to meet his requests for an extra selling assistant or a new fixture; the selling assistants who will be delighted with their higher individual takings and will be poised to do even better; the competitors who may have found their takings slightly down in their corresponding department. The manager will also have influenced others not included in his field of control: the other department managers in the branch who may want to find out whether they can learn something from him; and also other groups, within and outside the branch.

At the end of the first week, through this information/action interplay, the manager has created a new ongoing situation; the following week's situation will be organized so that it, in turn, becomes a strong foundation for the subsequent week's happenings; and so on. Every day, every week, the manager is with his staff, building and creating their work-situations to come.

Controlling

Controlling, the third strand of the managing process, is taking place as the coordinating is going on. Coordinating which, to repeat, is effective functional relating, generates its own control. The degree of co-relation *is* the measure of control. On the personal level, the individual gains more and more self-control as he intelligently coordinates and integrates his various tendencies. In the work-place, the better the reciprocal adjustings the manager can bring to the various activities involved in the task, the more effective *is* the control.

The job of managers is to coordinate facts, actual and potential, so that they can continuously adjust the ongoing activities to better fit them; more exactly, their job is to ingather relevant information from the operating field and disseminate it to the members of their groups so that together, individually and collectively and including the managers themselves, they adjust the task, whilst doing it, relative to the evolving situation. True coordination *is* control.

Controlling, therefore, blends with relating and coordinating to form the managing process which, for best working, must be continuous and anticipatory. Control, exercised after the event, at the end of the task, cannot obviously affect it. It may provide lessons for the future, assuming that the same conditions will always and exactly repeat themselves. As we live in increasing conditions of volatility and uncertainty, controls laid down on the basis of past history are unlikely to meet all the contingencies which arise in daily experience.

The continuous control inherent in the managing process does not, of course, preclude regular stocktakings to check performance and events, as means for managers to think through and visualize the future, better to see the evolving pattern and adjust today's business for tomorrow's needs.

The manager, through the managing process, unifies and integrates activities, always laying down today the foundation for tomorrow's future.

Requirements for Effective Managing

The functions of managers are very diverse. But, whether they are in production or distribution, in design or research, in marketing or planning, in finance or personnel, their basic function is always the same: to attain a given objective by a skilful combination and employment of the resources of people, money, materials and information, within a time scale laid down; in two words, to manage. Follett worked out the four underlying principles for effective managing as being: (1) reciprocal relating of all the factors in the situation; (2) direct communicating between the responsible people involved; (3) starting the process at the earliest stages; and (4) keeping it going on a continuing basis.

1 *Reciprocal relating of all the factors.*

The process of organizing resources is one of integration, not of aggregation. The manager, with his group, creates a whole – the finished task, the attained objective – out of the factors at their disposal. The essential nature of a unity is order. Order between sub-parts is one of relation, not of addition. It is a fallacy to hold that the whole is greater than its parts. The whole, the finished product whatever this may be, is different from, but not greater than, its constituent parts. When money, materials and people are combined together, the result is not a bit more of each, or a lot more of any one of them; the outcome is the performed task, something obviously quite different from any one of its inputs.

Take, for example, the company which suddenly finds that a competitor has brought out a product which directly competes with one of its main offerings. The directorial edict issued 'Reduce our price to 10 per cent below our competitor's' is merely a thoughtless reaction which may completely misdirect energies and actions.

The task in hand, how to respond successfully to the unexpected threat, is one of careful analysis of all the factors in the situation. The competing product has to be bought, broken down and subjected to minute examination. How are its parts put together? Where do they get them from? Are they made in-house or bought from outside? How much do they cost? What's the labour content cost? What's their likely profit margin per unit? What functions does the product fulfil? How is the product packaged, advertised, distributed? What are the offered payment terms? What's the level of after-sales service offered? And so on.

Each fact, each finding has to be analysed in relation to the others and also of course in relation to the company's own product. All the relevant departments – design, marketing, production, finance, personnel – have to work together. Each has its own competence which, combined with the others', will produce the best response-solution. There is a bit of clever designing here which we could copy. To implement this, we need to buy or lease a new machine; which is better? If to buy, have we got the money? Our component A is better than theirs, but their component B is functionally better than ours; where are they getting it from? Their labour costs appear lower than ours; why? Are we offering more functions in our product? Or is it because of our poor work organization? How many functions do our customers really need from the product: more or fewer? Are our competitors appealing to the same customer-segment as ours?

It is out of the interaction of this knowledge (which can be set out in a tree diagram) and of the consequential joint action that the company will evolve the right answer to the challenge: changing its offering so that, as a whole, in terms of functions, design, reliability, ease of purchase, payment terms, price, glamour, it meets its customers' requirements better than the new competing product. The customers themselves may now become a variable in the equation. The company may find it more profitable now to trade up (through additional functions and/or other changes in the marketing mix) or to trade down (through simplification of product, lower price and wider distribution). Before coming to the final decision, the company has to re-work the best value-transaction between its product (unchanged, traded up or down) and its customers, existing or potential, which now requires it to look at the whole of the competition, as changed by the new entrant.

It may be that the company, at the end of the day, does not have to change either the product or the price or the distribution network, having come to the conclusion, after the exhaustive study, that its product, as it is, is still ideal for its customer niche. It is only necessary to change its advertising and promotion strategy to emphasize the superiority of its product over the newcomer and to retain customer loyalty. However, the appearance of the competing product, on the face of it, changed the whole environment for the company which had, as a result, to review it as a whole, by re-examining all the factors in the new situation relative to each other, and not by looking at them, each in isolation and then sequentially.

Concentrating solely on any one factor – design or price, distribution network or advertising, functions or packaging – and excluding or subordinating the others to it narrows the field of control, reduces possibilities and opportunities and makes it unlikely (except by chance) to arrive at the right decisions and actions. It also means always reacting to events, instead of starting on the path of influencing and therefore controlling them.

2 *Direct contact between the responsible people involved.*
The most effective action results from direct communicating between the people who can influence the situation. Those directly involved in the making and marketing of the product have to get together, in the project team or task force, to pool their knowledge to arrive at the best joint answer. Neither the chief executive nor the heads of departments, separately or together, can impose the best solution, for it cannot be known until those who can find it have worked it out. The machine operator may have the best understanding of what his machine can do, in which case his presence in the project team will be more useful than that of the production manager,

in deciding whether a different machine is needed. The requirement is to establish *direct* relations between those who can contribute, so that there can be full and effective cross-fertilization of information and ideas.

3 *Starting at the earliest stages.*
The earlier the coordinating begins, the easier and more effectively is it achieved. The people studying the threat of the competing product will find the better answer more quickly, if they work together as a team from the very beginning. If the product went sequentially to design, then to production, then to marketing and so on, there could be no pooling and interaction of knowledge. The decision may have been tentatively reached that a new machine was required, only for it to be quashed when it went to the financial controller who decided that the existing machine was almost new and could not be scrapped. In sequential treatment, the responsible person in each department, having worked out his view on how to improve his piece of the action, would find it difficult to change it later, in response to the others. Views and attitudes harden and crystallize, so that mutual adjustments later are time-consuming and are made on the basis of compromise rather than integration.

4 *Coordinating as a continuous process.*
It is the continuity in the exchange of information leading to adjustments in activities which is the valuable factor. The competing product has created a problem for the company, because of its lack of anticipation and its inadequate relating with the competition. The alert, alive company would not have been caught napping in this way. It would have had the intelligence and the instinct to be aware of what their competitors were up to and would have anticipated the threat, by having the appropriate contingency plan ready. Continuous monitoring of the environment, internal and external, is a vital requirement for effective and successful managing.
Perhaps the best-known illustration of effective coordination is the Japanese *kan-ban* (just-in-time) method of production, where the manufacturers are in such close relations with their sub-contractors, through continuous reciprocal exchange of information, that neither they nor the sub-contractors have to build large stocks in anticipation of production. This obviously saves stockholding costs but in addition enables the Japanese manufacturers to respond more quickly to

changes in demand. The result is better customer satisfaction which gives the Japanese their competitive edge in the world market.

The Japanese working philosophy is different from that in Western countries. There, suppliers work exclusively for one manufacturer and their fortunes are wholly dependent on that manufacturer. In the UK and elsewhere in the West, the philosophy prevails of 'not putting all one's eggs in one basket'; neither manufacturer nor sub-contractor wants to be exclusively dependent on the other. The Japanese method cannot therefore be transplanted in its entirety into our different culture. However, its underlying principle of reciprocal exchange of information between all those involved in the task, flowing into coordinating action, can be emulated. It is nothing other – neither more nor less – than effective managing. The more successful of our companies, of course, do it all the time. It is just that little bit more difficult to achieve because, given the relative independence of the parties, coordination between them cannot be as close or continuous as in the Japanese set-up.

Trust as the Foundation Stone

An additional requirement for effective managing is that of trust. The managing process is interaction of information for the most effective action. For the exchange of information to be fullest, trust is of the essence: trust that the information will be used by each and everyone for the common purpose and not by one party for selfish ends. Trusting is risking that it may be so misused, but, to accomplish the task effectively, the risk has to be accepted. It has to be calculated, of course, but also taken. Trust cannot be imposed. It has to be learnt through practice, and earned.

If the existing situation is based on mistrusting relations, it cannot be changed, simply by decree. The ingrained habits of thought and of behaviour have to be changed through action. The managers, by virtue of their positions as leaders, have to be initiators in this respect: opening up the books, so to speak, to the members of their team and taking other steps to create better co-relatings.

A certain chief executive I know once gave up his car space in the company's car park to a junior subordinate for a temporary, specific situation, having worked out that this would better meet it. All the employees became aware that here was something new, a more egalitarian attitude in the making. Rank was not the determinant of privilege. Both rank and privilege were subordinate to the task in hand. Without fuss and with a small act which cost minimal personal inconvenience, the chief executive demonstrated the unity of purpose which joined them all. This small example began to change employee attitudes, gradually producing a more integrated effort and improved performance.

Trust has to be reciprocal. Managers cannot go on trusting, unless the managed respond with trust. Because of past experience, the response may be slow in coming. Managers have to persevere, perceptively and carefully, in the knowledge that trust begets trust. The leader leads, always by example; and actions always speak louder than words.

That intangible quality of trust the manager and the members of his team build between themselves enables that manager, in an emergency, where there is no time to explain or indeed to come to the best solution, to issue the command, the order, which will be unquestionably followed by the others; and, conversely, enables the members of the team, in the manager's absence, to act, because they know they are trusted to give of their best.

Field of Experience

Apart from trust which is basic to successful interaction, there should also be a commonality of experience between those involved in any endeavour. It is difficult to communicate otherwise, rather like attempting to relate without a common language. That department manager will be able to interact better with the buyer, if he shadows the buyer for a few days, learning about delivery time-lags, merchandise shortages and other similar contingencies; the buyer similarly would benefit by spending a little time in the selling department, finding out at first hand customers' reactions to certain items and understanding better the department manager's constraints of shortage of staff or poor fixturing. That sales manager would communicate better with the salespeople, if he went on the road with one of them, learning about the market, the customers, and the travelling schedules.

Sharing of experience is invaluable in creating real understanding between the managers and those in their teams. It increases joint knowledge and reduces fear. Managers getting the bright idea whilst shaving will get it that little bit more right, because of their experience in the field; subordinates will not be frightened to make a decision, because they know how their manager's mind works and know, as a result, what to do.

It is held that successful managers know how to handle people. This is true but it is only part, and therefore an incomplete description, of their function. Their job is much more intricate and exciting than that. They handle situations, where the people are but one of the factors – the most important factor, yes, but not the only one. Scientists, in their laboratory, can isolate and keep constant one or a few factors and then work out the effects of the others on them. Managers cannot do this. They can hold no factor constant. They have to connect and integrate them, as they are dynamically interacting and changing – much the more difficult job. And an integral element of the manager's job is the ability to resolve conflict constructively, a truly demanding task but always very satisfying in the performing.

Notes

1 A. Tillett, T. Kempner and G. Wills, eds, *Management Thinkers*, Pelican Books, London, 1978, p. 59.
2 Mary Parker Follett, *Creative Experience*, Peter Smith, New York, 1951, pp. 60, 63, 64.

4

Resolving Conflict: Integrating Differences

Conflict is generally regarded as a bad thing. Many people have a deep-rooted distaste for anything that may give rise to it. Some go to extremes and even tend to avoid discussion. 'I have given you my opinion; do what you like with it; I don't want to argue' a friend of mine invariably tells me; and yet a discussion is just what I would like to have, so that, arguing our different viewpoints, we might clarify and reconcile them.

Fear of conflict is often prevalent in the work-place; it is taken to spell trouble. Those who disagree with the general consensus are considered aggressive and disruptive; everyone must be of the same opinion. 'Don't rock the boat' is too often one of the tenets of managerial indoctrination. This was the constant refrain which friendly colleagues, taking me aside after board meetings at which I had unequivocally expressed my contrary views, would whisper to me. They meant well, but they were in error. Differences which are not aired gradually grow into resistance, difficult to deal with later; or, when completely suppressed, lead everyone to adopt exactly the same outlook, building that group-think mentality which is a pathological state of the group, auguring its entropy and creating the kind of corporate tunnel-vision which invites the impending take-over.

Conflict as Difference

Does conflict always need to be regarded as the expression of warfare and have, attached to it, connotations of fear and aggression? Should it not be thought of as the manifestation of difference – difference of opinions, of values, of interests? For that is what conflict starts by being: the expression of difference. In the context of the work-place, this may mean differences between employer and employees; those between directors or between managers, or between workers on the shop floor.

These differences need not be regarded, in themselves, as dangerous or destructive; on the contrary, they could be capitalized. When discussing the health of the group, in chapter 2, we saw that its well-being depended on difference. If people's interests always remained identical, life would stagnate. Diversity is the most essential feature of life and fear of difference is dread of life itself. Conflict is a fact of life. Instead of prejudging it as 'bad' and suppressing it, we could accept it openly and make it work for us. Treated as the expression of legitimate difference, it can be used as the spur to find the wider solution, the solution that will meet the mutual interests of the parties involved in it. Follett put the case for understanding and exploiting conflict:

As conflict – difference – is here in the world, as we cannot avoid it, we should, I think, use it. Instead of condemning it, we should set it to work for us. Why not? What does the mechanical engineer do with friction? Of course, his chief job is to eliminate friction, but it is also true that he also capitalises friction . . . The friction between the driving wheel of the locomotive and the track is necessary to haul the train. The music of the violin we get by friction. We talk of the friction of mind on mind as a good thing. So in business, too, we have to know when to try to eliminate friction and when to try to capitalise it, when to see what work we can make it do . . . We can set conflict to work and make it *do* something for us.[1]

Thus, to welcome conflict is not to welcome an unending dispute between incompatibles.

Dealing with Conflict

Our attitude to conflict determines the way we deal with it. The traditional view is to see it as erupting between competing interests, between parties in the adversarial fight set. Domination or compromise is used as the means of coping with it. Either of these methods, based on the relative powers of the conflicting parties, merely *settles* the conflict; neither *resolves* it. There is a third way – integration – which, based on the concept of joining powers instead of setting them against each other, provides the better long-lasting solution; and yet it is seldom used. It is worthwhile considering in some detail the three main alternatives.

1 *Domination.*

Perhaps this is the easiest way of settling a conflict, if one has the power and can use it. But, even where it is applied successfully, the resulting victory is a victory of the moment only. At best, the victors can keep the other side down by additional doses of domination, but the time comes, sooner rather than later these days, when they can no longer sustain the effort; or the weak party builds up its own strength and gets the better of the other side.

I had an early experience of this. In my first post as a director of buying, I had in my directorate a central buyer with a very large buying power. When I first accompanied him in some of his buying trips, I was surprised at the way he dealt with the small manufacturers, the ones just starting out and badly needing our business. He would tell them that the item was no good, that the leather was poor, the machining too loose, the studs inferior and the lining badly put in; 'but I'll give you an order for it; I'll give you £x for it and I want 5,000 in this colour combination, to be delivered by . . . This is my last word. Take it or leave it'.

The suppliers would invariably take it. I could not understand why our buyer was buying an article he thought so defective. Wasn't he letting our customers down? What would this do to our reputation?

'Oh, no' he would explain patiently 'the article is really first-class, better-made than the one I am getting from X. In fact, I am going to sell it at a price which will give me double the profit on it that I get on X's item'.

'Then, why are you screwing him down to the ground on the price?' I would ask, nonplussed.

'That's the way to treat them; show them who's the boss; keep them under control', he, somewhat patronizingly, would show me the ways of staying on top in business.

This buyer had a real nose for merchandise. He had the flair and the ability to ferret out the up-and-coming suppliers who were better attuned to fashion trends, but struggling to get a foothold in the market. He got them – but he did not keep them. They accepted his orders, because it was their only alternative to not selling at all. As a result of dealing with our buyer, they did get a foothold in the market.

Their merchandise got displayed in the best shops in the most important towns and it sold well. And it was seen by our competitors; thus alerted, it would not take them long to find the makers and, offering them better terms than our buyer did, would filch them from us. We quickly lost these promising sources of supply.

I did not like this buyer's attitude towards our small suppliers. Essentially, it offended my sense of fairness. Yet, I did not want to appeal to fairness, for I did not want to be subjected to a lecture on 'what's fair in business', the theoretical discussion of which would have simply ended in our becoming more hardened in our respective views. I wanted to prove to him that unfairness simply did not work. So, I delved into his performance and showed him the analyses I made of the turnover in his new suppliers in the previous three years. He was losing them at the same rate as he was gaining new ones. There was a steady rise in his turnover and good profitability, but not the dramatic increase that would flow, if he succeeded in keeping a larger proportion of them.

'Why don't you just try, with that bright young supplier, the one you think best, just to accept his price, or even bowl him over by adding a couple of pence to it? And why do you want to double your profit on his merchandise relative to that of the well-established manufacturer? If you sold the item at a profit margin nearer your average, you could sell double the quantity and your total profit would be much larger. Here are the figures I have worked out. What do you think? Why don't you try this way for a change and see how it works?'

I don't think he thought much of my business acumen (What? Offering a higher price than the supplier demanded?) but the work I had put into the exercise made him decide that he had perhaps better humour his new director. The result, however, soon convinced him. Sales of the item, at the lower price which still gave us a healthy profit, zoomed up, making for substantial repeat orders. Just as important, he got the allegiance of that supplier who would not, thereafter, sell anything to our competitors without first offering it to him. Little by little, this buyer followed the same strategy with the new small suppliers he was discovering. Having these at the back of him gave him the strength to negotiate better terms with his main suppliers. Turnover in his department shot up and so did his profitability. From the reasonably good buyer he had been, he developed into a first-class operator, fully capitalizing on his merchandise flair, through not taking advantage of his small suppliers. He learned that domination was not the best way to get their willing cooperation.

People learn, sometimes slowly and painfully, through playing every move, through actual experience, the waste and futility of establishing their claims through domination.

2 *Compromise.*

When people learn that domination does not work, they move to compromising. Compromise is thought of as a 'good' thing – reasonable, sensible; it is invariably advocated to the warring parties. 'Find a compromise' was the advice given even by the church leaders to both the Coal Board and the miners, during their bitter battle in 1984. When differences which have been allowed to smoulder finally erupt into open conflict, everyone scurries round to find a compromise. Very often, it is sought by the conflicting parties themselves.

Compromise inevitably involves each side giving up something of its own demand. To avoid this, the parties play the bargaining game. They 'doctor' their claims, the one asking for much more than it is prepared to accept and the other offering less than it is prepared to concede. Each side is working from the premise that it will emerge with its real demand still intact, after the bargaining manoeuvres. This is possible, where the powers of the two parties are relatively equally matched, where compromise may result in some kind of give-and-take accommodation. If the mutual exchange is of the bits, put in or kept out as bargaining counters, why all the waste of time and energy spent on the bargaining? Of course, the parties themselves do not view the situation in this way; each thinks that, by clever manoeuvring, it will get the better bargain. There is also the excitement of fighting and winning. Even defeat is exciting: it recharges the adrenalin of the loser who immediately starts preparing himself for the next fight, when he can plan to be the winner.

Respective powers are, however, seldom equally matched at the time of the conflict. Very often, the party which thinks it is in the stronger position will choose the time and place to do battle, to take advantage of the other. Like domination, bargaining is based on power, and the relative strengths of the parties to the dispute will usually determine the result. This will not always be apparent. Faces may be saved; both sides may emerge from the negotiating room claiming a victory for common sense or some such cliché but, each knows, if no one else does, who has been the victor in the proceedings: the one who wielded the greater power at that conjunction of circumstances.

Compromise is of course preferable to straightforward domination, the imposed solution, but it is neither efficient nor effective. If one thinks carefully about it, it is not right in principle and it does not work in practice over the long-term either. It is not right in principle because if one thinks that what one wants is right and fair, why should one give up any part of it? And compromise does not work in practice either, because the differences are not truly resolved. They are merely ironed out, in a framework of mistrust and ambiguity, in a settlement which leaves many of them hazy and unsettled. So often, there is disagreement over a settlement which has only just been signed by both parties; each interprets it differently and claims their interpretation to be the right one; so often does the settlement itself become the source of further conflict.

The fact is that, like domination, compromise has in it the seeds of its own destruction. After the settlement, each side will seek to consolidate his position, and every such effort will be seen by the other as an attempt to upset the agreed equilibrium. Mistrust and resentment grow. The same conflict or another, more acute, arises sooner or later. Compromise provides peace, of a kind. It is in essence an expedient only, a palliative and a temporary one at that.

3 Integration.

Compromise need not be, and is not, the only alternative to domination. There is a third way to resolve differences, and that is by integration. Integration occurs, Follett explained, when a solution is found that allows both interests to find their place in it and when neither party sacrifices anything of significance to him.

Follett's celebrated personal example of integration, of finding the integrative solution which meets the needs of both parties, has often been quoted and is worth repeating. She tells of an occasion in the Harvard Library when she wanted the window shut whilst someone else in the room wanted it open. All the makings of a dispute, but:

We opened the window in the next room, where no one was sitting. This was not a compromise, because there was no curtailment of desire; we both got what we really wanted. For I did not want a closed room, I simply did not want the north wind to blow directly on me; likewise, the other occupant did not want that particular window open, he merely wanted more air in the room.[2]

I well remember my first conscious effort at finding the integrative solution. The central display manager was sitting in my office and we were discussing the location boards in the store. The central rule was that departments had to be listed in alphabetical order. So, he was insisting that Baby Linens (which were not in much demand then, few people having babies at that time) had to come first. I wanted Young Fashions (very buoyant and all hidden on the top floor) to come first. I was invoking my authority as general manager, getting set in the adversarial mode; we were approaching a bad-tempered deadlock. And then, I thought: 'He's only trying to implement the rules. Which could be the solution that would meet his need and, at the same time, mine? I had hardly formulated the question that I found the answer. 'How about calling that top floor department *All Young Fashions?*' He was delighted, for, as the name of the department now started with A, he could put it right at the top of the list on the boards, without derogating from the central rule. I, too, was delighted for I also got what I wanted. A potentially explosive situation was defused and became the plank for the subsequent cooperative relationship between us.

These examples, relatively insignificant in themselves, illustrate, nevertheless, the attitude of mind that has to be developed, if a conflict is not merely to be *settled*, but *resolved*. Integration is not, of course, always possible. There are irreconcilables in life, but it is possible to achieve it much more often than we think. Given the right frame of mind and the appropriate techniques, we can learn to accommodate each other's needs and interests in small things, without loss to either; as we gain experience in the use of the method, we become better at it and better prepared to manage the bigger problems when they appear.

Follett was advocating, over seventy years ago, the use of integration as the most productive method of resolving conflict. But we remain stuck, in the main, at the bargaining stage. I attended a seminar not so long ago, where a professor of marketing distributed a list with two hundred bargaining tactics to use in negotiations, from 'acting crazy' (put on a good show by visibly demonstrating your emotional commitment to your position) to 'creating surprises' (keep the opponent off balance by a drastic, dramatic, sudden shift in your tactics in general) to 'remaining unpredictable' (keep the opponent from anticipating your moves).

There are indications that we are moving forward, evolving to the more productive and satisfying method of integration. Here and there, greater discrimination is shown in distinguishing between distributive bargaining (sharing the cake) from integrative bargaining (increasing the cake), with emphasis on the latter. There is a trend towards the principled approach to negotiation. Centres for Conflict Resolution have sprung up, in the academic field, to study mainly international conflict. In the UK, the Centre for the Analysis of Conflict, founded in 1965, is now well established at the University of Kent at Canterbury. Its techniques for resolving international conflict in diverse situations, including communal violence, insurrection and war are very much those Follett was teaching in the 1920s, as applicable in any field where conflict arises.

In the USA, where litigation has become a way of life, a number of the Fortune 500 companies decided, in the mid 1970s, to find a better way than that wasteful and unwieldy process. They came up with the concept of the 'alternative dispute resolution' where the parties in the dispute have themselves to be directly involved in shaping the solution. They make informal presentations in joint session under the neutral leadership of a third party and these are then followed by 'caucuses' where they enter into open and frank discussions about the merits and the downside of their case. Here again, the underlying principle of integrating differences and the techniques used of direct and frank discussions are those advocated by Follett seventy years ago.

These harbingers of change, encouraging as they are, unfortunately remain the exception. They have not yet percolated through into wider general usage. Integration as the better means of resolving conflict is still too rare. Yet, integration is very much the modern concept. In computer technology, for example, it is the key to bringing about effective connections. We could use the notion in our everyday affairs equally effectively to integrate our differences. The method is used anyway, when we work within the cooperative framework. The need is to extend its use in areas of incipient or actual conflict; to study and develop the art of integration, making it an integral part of our habits of thought and action, so that it replaces compromise which is, after all, but an intermediary step in our social evolution. The need is not for lists and books on how to get the better of the other party by childish and undignified stratagems but for advice on how to integrate for all to win – much the more intelligent and wiser approach.

The Techniques for Integration

The bargaining that goes on in seeking a compromise settlement to conflict has become something of a fine art, with techniques that are well established and predictably used. Those for finding the integrative solution are very different. They involve developing the joint approach; putting all one's cards on the table and treating the conflict as a problem to be solved by the parties themselves.

1 *Evolving the joint approach.*

Most, if not all, people who go to the committee meeting or the conference room, go with preconceived ideas of what the other side wants, a firm definition of their own objectives and their minds made up. They form a shrewd idea of the ploys the other side will adopt and have their own counter-moves planned. Thus, they go in, all set for a fight, and a fight there is, until someone suggests a compromise. That is no way to resolving opposing views or competing interests on a satisfactory and relatively permanent basis.

The more intelligent approach is 'Let's see what the real problem is and how we can solve it together.' It creates a totally different operating framework in which both parties can distance themselves from the conflict and depersonalize the issue; in this way, they are better able to examine it objectively, as a problem to the solution of which both can and will contribute. The imperative here is that both parties feel and accept that it will redound to their respective mutual benefit to abandon the adversarial mode for the cooperative one.

This approach is not always easy to get going, entrenched as people emotionally become in the merits of their case. Pride and prejudice often stand in the way. Clearly, it is better if the parties can come together in that spirit to begin with – they will be almost half way home. But this is not a *sine qua non*. In minor conflicts, it can be sufficient for just one of the parties to show willing. We influence each other. If one party is determined to cooperate, the other will find it difficult not to respond in the same way. One's goodwill can almost compel the other to reciprocate. At the extreme, if I find the solution which meets your demand without compromising my own, and I offer it to you, what else is left for us to fight about?

Through its own initiatives, through its own actions, one party can often secure in return the cooperation of the other party, previously combative. The good managers will resolve many of the conflicts with which they are faced in this way. The very good managers will anticipate conflict, not by avoiding it, but playing the game differently, like the first-class chess players who anticipate the configuration of moves and counter-moves and go straight to the action which will give them the advantage. It is always the manager's privilege, as the leader, to start the cooperating ball rolling. And, in complete deadlock, apparent failure need not always be accepted as final. The services of a third party, outside the actual conflict, can often be enlisted with success.

2 *Uncovering the differences.*

Part of the art of bargaining is to refuse to show one's hand; to select those facts advantageous to one's case and forget the others; to obscure the issues; to leave things fudged and ambiguous; to create room for manoeuvring. 'Keep something up your sleeve' was the constant advice given me, to which I would sometimes jokingly reply that, not wearing men's shirts, I did not have the right sleeves to keep anything in. To keep the other side guessing and to table the trump card at the right psychological moment is the essence of the game. With both sides following the same strategy, it degenerates into a battle of wits, in which one side outsmarts the other, or deadlock results. The first outcome, for ethical and practical reasons, reflects no credit on the perpetrating party; the second spells trouble.

The techniques for integration stand at the opposite of those involved in bargaining. If a lasting solution is genuinely being sought, then the first step is for both sides to put their cards on the table, clearly and unambiguously to set their demand or offer and give their reasons for it. By bringing their respective positions into the open and doing this together, they are putting them in the one field of vision, in the same frame, in the same picture which will enable them to see them side by side that more realistically, that more fully. Conflicts of interest are also subjective matters. Differences between individuals and groups are not only differences of so-called objective facts; they also include differences in values, in feelings, in prejudices – and these are a feature of the conflict. In putting all their cards on the table, each party is getting to know something of the background attaching to the facts of the other; in the interplay of setting its case down and justifying its position, each is also giving the other the opportunity to learn about these intangibles, knowledge of a very important kind which will not only help at the outset but in the subsequent stages as well.

As a merchandise director, leading a large number of buyers, I did not have the specialism that each buyer had in respect of his merchandise category. My contribution to help them do their job better was to indoctrinate them with the value of putting all their cards on the table: 'Take your suppliers into your confidence. Tell them your intended selling prices. They find them out anyway, by walking into any one of our shops, a few weeks later. If you tell them your mark-up, you might work a better price together. If they reduced their price to you by £x, you could reduce yours to your customers by perhaps £2x; sales could increase by so much per cent. The manufacturers would get repeat orders; your total profit would be higher; so would theirs; and you would be satisfying more customers, those who wouldn't buy at the higher price. To achieve all this, you have to work with your suppliers, join with them to make the best offer to the customer.

'You get a great deal of merchandise information on Monday mornings. Why don't you ring your suppliers of the best-sellers and tell them exactly how you have sold them in the previous week – stockturn, and sales by size, colour and geographical pattern? In this way, if you want to place a repeat order the following week, the suppliers will have been alerted to the likely situation and perhaps made provisional bookings for materials and manufacturing time.

'The same applies to your poor sellers. You'll know why they have not sold. Let the manufacturers know. If it is a question of colour or size and you have got another order for the same item in the pipeline, they may not have started processing the order and together you could change the size assortment, and perhaps the colour combinations. If it is a question of shape, the garment could perhaps be re-shaped, if it has not gone into production yet.'

All this was strange to the buyers at first. They had been trained to play the game with their cards close to their chest, giving very little information away to their suppliers, for fear that they would use it against them, in their negotiations, or that they would pass it to our competitors to whom they also sold. Quite ridiculous and unwarranted fears, for both suppliers and competitors could just walk into our shops and see for themselves, from a cursory look at the rails, what was selling and not selling. That's just what I did in keeping my tabs on what our competitors were doing; so did the buyers when they visited their competitors' outlets.

It took time to inculcate the new attitude but it got implanted. The new openness worked wonders, sending sales and profits up. It also changed the manufacturers' attitudes towards the buyers. They started taking the initiative themselves, warning them that this colour, that shape, that size were not selling well and suggesting changes. In some cases, where the relationship between manufacturer and buyer had blossomed into one of complete trust, the manufacturers would themselves take the responsibility for making some changes to the order, if the buyer was away or they couldn't get the immediate decision needed. They started themselves suggesting price reductions or offering to accept a lower mark-up to enable the buyer to purchase merchandise which, otherwise, would have been outside his price structure.

Thus, our cards-on-the-table policy was generally fully reciprocated by the manufacturers. Together, we established an identity of interests which included that of the customer. This paid off handsomely, not only in terms of higher profit but also on delivery dates which became more reliable or, when supplies were tight, allowed us first call on them.

This cards-on-the-table policy, applied in all the relationships within the buying group: between the buyer and the members of his team, between buyers, between their teams, and also in its relations with the other groups in the company as well as with the customers. All this created an exciting and professional environment, where there were no Monday morning blues, where Monday was in fact the most lively day in the week, when everybody came early, wanting to get first hold of those computer reports to get the detail of the figures and to start the action going.

In the most technologically advanced companies, such merchandise information is now directly available to the suppliers, being included in their integrated information systems. It presupposes of course full cards-on-the-table disclosure, a large step forward. It is invaluable as a tool to facilitate personal communicating; however, it cannot wholly replace it.

3 *Comparing the issues.*

When the respective requirements of the parties are studied in detail jointly, when they are broken down in their constituent parts, there can be a comparison of interests which can lead to costless exchanges. The top priority in your list of demands may rank very low in mine. I am indifferent whether I surrender or retain it. The converse situation may apply to my demands: my top priority ranks very low with you. Thus, a fair exchange of values can be achieved, at no sacrifice to either. This will apply generally down the whole scale of priorities, as no two parties will have the same scale of preferences in every situation. Each exchange leads to a revaluation of all the remaining interests which, in its turn, facilitates further similar cost-free exchanges.

It is also possible, by breaking down the whole demand, to go behind the ostensible demand, behind the declared motive, to get at the real demand and the underlying motive. If the marketing manager is at odds with the production manager, it is usually found that neither's declared interest is the significant feature of the conflict but the outside interest – that of the market – is the demand which they must look at together and satisfy.

Accurate analysis of the underlying causes of the conflict, of which the parties themselves may not have been aware but which they uncover in the process of studying the problem together, changes the situation and helps the parties to find answers to it. Analysis and resolution go together. If workers are asking for more money or for a reduction in working hours, the manager may find that what they truly want is more autonomy in their work and that the declared demand is the only way they can think of, to get compensation for the frustration endured at work. The manager may be able to reorganize the work and thus meet their real demand; or the manager may find that they are asking for more money because the existing working conditions – late deliveries of essential materials, obsolete machinery – are preventing them from earning what they could earn without these impediments; by removing these, the real need can be satisfied.

Basic misunderstandings can and do occur. The marketing people tell production that they must be able to produce a particular item at a given price, as the competition is doing it. The production people cannot do it, as they have to buy their main materials from a subsidiary at higher prices than the competitors are paying for theirs in the open market. Both marketing and production are right, on their own given facts. When they get together and find the reason for their difference, they can work to solve this sub-problem first; resolving it may wholly resolve their conflict.

Semantics can always be a problem. The British billion used to be different from its American counterpart; the same words hold different meanings for different people. Faulty encoding and decoding can also give rise to another kind of misunderstanding. The story is well-known of the embattled platoon which sent the message: 'Are going to advance. Send reinforcements' received as 'Are going to a dance. Send three and fourpence'. These difficulties which quickly escalate are cleared up more easily, when the opposing parties meet face to face, speak their minds and make themselves clearly and fully understood.

4 *Creating and inventing.*

The methods of the joint approach, of bringing out the differences into the open, of evaluating together the issues relative to each other may provide the solution. But, sometimes, the impasse of two entrenched irreconcilable positions is reached. The thing to avoid then is the trap of the 'either-or' syndrome: 'Either I now get my way or I lose everything; how can I now get my way?' The technique here is to change one's field of vision, to seek the different picture in which the respective positions of the parties fall in differently where they can be adjusted for a better fit. More often than not, this shifting of vision enables the parties to project their minds beyond the impasse and to reorientate their thinking; it refocuses it so that it alights on the problem from a different angle and illuminates it differently and, in the process, points out to a series of steps which thread the way out of the deadlock.

It may sound rather difficult and, to some hard-bitten managers, even fanciful, but it does work and it improves with practice. It requires an open mind, imagination and creativeness, but it is exciting. It is also infectious. The other side tends to get excited when it sees the plus-value of such inventiveness and responds in the same way, perhaps with even greater originality and creative new-look thinking. And so the impasse opens and the path found to the fuller answer, the long-lasting solution which both parties have jointly found and which is truly theirs, for they have created it.

5 *Calling in a third party.*

The intervention of a third party has been mentioned. In some ways, it may appear an admission of defeat: the ACAS fall-back prop; a confession of intransigence; a lack of management skill on one side or the other, or both. But it need not necessarily be so. It may be that the very complexities of the case lift it beyond the capacities of the parties concerned to solve it unaided; or the third party may be needed because the conflict has gone so far that relations between the parties have practically broken down and outside help is required to repair their relationship sufficiently to get them to sit together at the same table again.

The function of this third party has to be seen as neutral by both. It is a resource available to both of them to get going again, and to keep going. The third party may provide a meeting place outside their own territory, where they can do their confronting in a less emotionally-charged environment; they may provide information from their knowledge and experience which, injected during the proceedings, may open a way through the dead ends they will encounter. The third parties are neither umpires nor arbitrators. Their value comes from being completely outside the conflict, assiduously remaining outside it and being perceived by the opponents as unbiased, favouring neither one nor the other. They are facilitators, available impartially to both of them, to enable them to work out their own solution.

The solution, when found, must be that which the sides in conflict would themselves have worked out, not one pressed upon them by the third party, even if that third party is an expert or higher authority. This is extremely important: an imposed settlement, however delicately manipulated, is no true solution.

Managers, in their daily work, do not have to manage many mega-conflicts; but they can use a facilitator at the approach of an impasse. If they cannot find the integrative solution, they may have got stuck in the 'either-or' syndrome. Discussing the problem with someone outside it, someone whose judgement they trust and who may have wider or different knowledge and experience, will put the problem in yet a different perspective and may well show the way. How often, for example, does one's spouse, through asking questions and giving a point of view, both totally unrelated apparently to the facts of the case, show the way to the elusive answer?

6 *Integrating other interests.*

It is not sufficient for the conflicting parties to integrate solely their respective interests. They need to have regard to those of connecting groups. The conflicting parties do not operate in a vacuum but within a web of other groups whose interests will be different from, or may clash with, theirs. It is in studying the whole field of interests that they can accommodate theirs within it. It is in knowing how these various interests interlink and affect each other that they can achieve a better dynamic order between them and find their rightful places in it.

Producers who combine together to give themselves an advantage over the buyers of their products may gain superiority, but for a short time only. They themselves create the situation which compels the others to find ways and means to circumvent their monopoly. Even in the extreme case of the oil crisis of 1973, the users, by saving energy and using other fuels, reduced their oil consumption with a consequential fall in the price of oil. Directors who boost their pay by awarding themselves (shareholders' approval being in most cases a formality) bonuses, share options and extravagant perks, without sufficient regard of their effect on the work-force enjoined to restrain its wage demands, are being short-sighted. Their actions will only be reciprocated by claims for higher wages and/or resentment and non-cooperation, all of which leads to lower profitability of the business, making the company vulnerable to take-over. Trade unions who clamour for higher wages without offering higher productivity and without regard for the state of the market make for more capital-intensive operations and loss of employment for their own members.

In every case, the interests of the conflicting parties are only part of the picture; along with their own interests they have to take account of those of the others. For the company, this means integrating the interests of all parties connected with it: employees (both managers and managed), customers, shareholders, suppliers, bankers, government and public opinion, without favouring any one group at the expense of the others. Each has to be allotted its fair share. Each has to have its proper place in the overall canvas.

The Plus Value of Constructive Conflict

Conflict is integral to living. Our desires are innumerable and some clash with others. The persons who love fattening foods and yet want to remain slim and healthy learn to reconcile these two contrary desires by subordinating the former to the latter which they value more highly. They assess their relative costs and benefits and resolve the problem on the basis of the best net value to themselves, their own best self-interest. There is no sacrifice, for they are putting conflicting desires in their proper relative order and, as a result, becoming better integrated, radiating strength and confidence. The individuals who do not succeed in resolving the same internal conflict are unhappy and feel inadequate; as a result, they are less sure in their relations with others. Being less well-balanced, they are letting themselves down. It is the conflicting desires, wants, aims in the individual and between individuals and groups that make living an interesting and worthwhile challenge. Without these tensions and frictions, without this competition, we could not go forward; atrophy would set it.

Conflict is unresolved difference. Some differences are absolutely incompatible. There is an irreconcilable difference of view between the person, pointing a gun at me to shoot me dead, and myself, who have no desire to lose my life. There are other less dramatic disagreements in life, but no less incompatible for that. There is tragedy in life; there will always be. But differences can be reconciled much more often than we think. France and Germany were enemies for a long time; they resolved their differences when they developed a wider vision and integrated their interests in it; each is now the stronger for that. The USSR and the USA, in 1990, are on the road to achieving a friendly *modus vivendi* – something that was inconceivable only a few years earlier. In late 1989, a combative union enjoined its members in the car industry to increase their productivity – an unprecedented occurrence.

As we learn not to be fearful of conflict, we can meet it and resolve it in its early stages, before it has had time to develop into entrenched and unshiftable positions. We fear difference for many reasons, mainly perhaps because of our fear of the unknown. 'The thing you know is better than the thing you don't know', 'Let sleeping dogs lie' reflect the apathetic streak in human nature. It is the opposite instinct – curiosity, the need to know, to understand, so as to do and control – which shows the true potential of human nature and takes us forward.

Opposites are complementary; they can be brought together for each to provide its relevant virtue to their joint combination. As we learn to see difference and conflict as something positive, something that can yield us value, we become less fearful of them and can welcome them. It is our attitude towards them, what we make of them, how we use them, that makes them 'good' or 'bad'.

Conflict is unproductive, when settled by domination or compromise, on the basis of the zero-sum theory which says that the gain of one must equal the loss of the other; when the rules of the noughts and crosses game are used, with the number of moves strictly given and with a winner and a loser at the end.

It is made productive when resolved by the method of integration, on the basis of the positive-sum theory, where we can find the solution that turns both us and the others involved in the situation into winners. This is not beyond the wit of man. It is a method applicable in every field involving social relations, in the home, in industry, in business, in government, in international affairs.

Conflict, used constructively, is the way to progress. The scientist creates conflict by refuting the *status quo*, rejecting the existing theory as limited in its explanation and envisioning and producing the wider theory, the more integrative solution that encompasses explanations of matters previously left unexplained. His better answer now becomes the *status quo* and remains so until another scientist, dissatisfied with it, challenges it and finds still the wider solution. And so, the sum of knowledge is increased and the human race progresses.

The really successful marketers are the pioneers who play the game differently; they do not compete blow for blow against the others. They search and find a need in the market which is not being met and which they set out to satisfy. They build their own niche, thus enlarging the whole market for that product or service. They actually create difference in order to capitalize on it.

As with the inventive marketer or scientist, so too managers in their work-place can capitalize on the plus-values of difference and conflict. Both can be put to work and used as welcome opportunities to search and find the better solution, the one that will meet more fully the existing interests of all concerned.

The solution that is found for today's conflict is not permanent. No one can remain complacent. The environment changes; one's respective needs and interests change. The fact that a conflict has been resolved today does not mean that new differences will not arise next week, next month, next year. They will, for life is ongoing and the *status quo* is only temporary. As domination and compromise carry in them the seeds of their own destruction, so is disintegration the opposite of integration. Integration stabilizes but cannot fix a situation for very long. It carries, however, its own positive momentum; as well as resolving the present conflict, it provides the base for the better resolution of future conflicts; the understanding and the practice we gain from resolving our disagreements today makes it easier to integrate our differences tomorrow.

Follett had an interesting phrase. She said that we could move to 'progressive differings' and put it in her usual down-to-earth manner:

We can often measure our progress by watching the nature of our conflicts. Social progress is in this respect like individual progress; we become spiritually more and more developed as our conflicts rise to higher levels. If a man should tell you that his chief daily conflict within himself is 'Shall I steal or not steal?' you would know what to think of his stage of development . . . In the same way, one test of your business organisation is not how many conflicts you have, for conflicts are the essence of life, but what are your conflicts. And how do you deal with them?

And she finished with a clear declaration of her concept of constructive conflict:

It is to be hoped that we shall not always have strikes, but it is equally to be hoped that we shall always have conflict, the kind that leads to invention, to the emergence of new values.[3]

Conflict, anathema to so many of our weaker brethren, can be the path to progress and understanding.

I remember very clearly my first year in general management in the business arena. 'Don't put all your cards on the table; keep something up your sleeve' implored my colleagues and friends. I instinctively rebelled against what I felt simply did not make sense. How could I get what I wanted if I did not declare it in its full detail? 'But A has a Machiavellian mind; he'll run rings round you; don't tell him everything'; or 'You're not dealing any longer with professional people; the suppliers will take you for a ride in no time at all, if you show them your hand.' These advisers were equating openness and straightforwardness with naivety and foolishness. But I knew I was not stupid and I felt I could hold my own with the wiliest of suppliers or those in the company with the most recondite minds.

The so-called rogue suppliers turned out to have a very limited repertoire of tactics, at most ten (nothing like those two hundred ways that professor of marketing had so patiently, and in my view so uselessly, collected) and I would jokingly tell them to go and find something a little more fanciful to entertain me with. More seriously, I would say to them: 'Please cut the cackle and come to the point. I have told you what we want. Why don't you tell me exactly what you need to make out of this transaction and what you can or cannot do? Perhaps I can help by adjusting our own requirements.' More than price, it was deliveries that bedevilled our relations with suppliers.

Over-optimism seems to be inherent in the breed. So, it was a question here of finding out whether they had, or when they would get, the cloth, and the lining and the buttons and the thread and the manufacturing time and so on, working out with them a delivery date they could effectively keep. A different working relationship was established and we got the deliveries on time. There were no more fires in the factory and typhoons in Hong Kong, providing them with *forces majeures* for delivery-time extensions and we were not left in the lurch without merchandise at the time they had undertaken to deliver.

As for those with Machiavellian minds, I enjoyed sparring with them. My purpose was to find the better way, not to impose my viewpoint and, if they could convince me that I was wrong in whole or in part, well and good. Here, too, I could not see the point of being economical with the truth as I saw it, for, if I did not tell them exactly what I thought or knew, how could they convince me of the error of my ways? And it wasn't all one way. As they could convince me that they were right sometimes, so could I convince them that I was right at other times. It seems that instinctively I was following the integrative approach, but without knowing its underlying concept. So, it was a delight for me to come across Follett's idea of constructive conflict.

Interestingly enough, there appears to be a parallel in the way Jewish religious students study the *Talmud*, the Law. The study has to be done in pairs and the mode is adversarial, each party arguing for the correctness of his interpretation and wanting to win. But the rule is that, should one of them be unable to progress his argument further and wishes to declare himself beaten, the other cannot accept his submission if he knows the way out of his opponent's impasse; in such a case, he has to show him the way out, so that they can proceed with further argumentation. The end aim is to win – but on the basis of their best joint capacity to unravel the most cogent interpretation. This is not the end of the affair, for they must submit their findings to the scrutiny of their teacher who may yet offer them a possibility to argue further and send them back to the drawing board. And no interpretation can ever be final, even when delivered by the most prestigious rabbinical scholar. It has, of course, the authority of its author but it is essentially a guideline to others to pursue their own search. This surely sharpens the mind and must make the exercise intellectually absorbing and exciting. It is competition embedded in cooperation – an unbeatable formula. This method strikes me as not very different from that which Popper put forward to explain, through conjectures and refutations, scientific progress.

The manager who welcomes difference, who accepts conflict as a fact of life, without pre-judging it as good or bad, can use both constructively and turn them into a very good thing: the creative and productive work-group.

I myself have tried over the years to practise, with varying degrees of success, the integrative-solution approach in conflictual situations. The phrase 'Seek the integrative solution' has been a kind of mantra to me, the passwords that have opened the way out of many a cul-de-sac in personal, professional and business relations. I can vouch that it is most rewarding and productive and fun. I recommend it without reservation.

The other great advantage of this method of resolving conflict is that it helps to develop individual powers and to combine them into the total power of the team, a truly dynamic force that enables it to achieve its tasks with 'gusto and with feeling', to use one of my recent slogans.

Notes

1 Mary Parker Follett, *Dynamic Administration: the Collected Papers of Mary Parker Follett*, Elliott M. Fox and L. Urwick, eds, Pitman Publishing, London, 1973, pp. 1–2.
2 Follett, *Dynamic Administration*, p. 3.
3 Follett, *Dynamic Administration*, pp. 6–7.

5

Growing Joint Power:
Power-with, Not Power-over

Power is one of the most significant factors in the lives of individuals, groups and nations. It determines a nation's position in international relations; a person's place in society. All in their different spheres seek to achieve power and to exercise it in pursuit of their aims and aspirations; all, in the long run, find themselves circumscribed by superior power exercised or threatened by others with conflicting aims. To achieve power and hang on to it is the motivating force in all political activity. The rise and rise of groups, one of the most significant social trends of the last few decades, is due to the desire of ordinary individuals to have more power and to exercise it more directly. They organize themselves in groups for the express purpose of furthering their interests and ensuring their rightful slice of the cake. They organize for power.

Empowerment, the relatively new buzz-word with a large future, has increased awareness of the virtues of power. Power is no longer accepted as the prerogative of the few. Like foreign travel, it is becoming democratized. The old-established and recognized powers of state, church and army or those of vested interests, such as big business, trade union or entrenched profession, are themselves becoming increasingly subject to the new rising powers: media power, ethical power, green power, female power, terrorist power. Above all, the conscious use of power has spread to the people; no longer mere crowds, rushing to the barricades and easily dispersible, but disciplined and determinedly non-violent, massive groups, they are, startlingly, changing political systems, dramatically illuminating the powerlessness of leaders who do not deliver the goods, be they political or economic.

As with the political leader who is discarded when no longer effective, so with the manager. As leader, he too has to deliver. This is his function. If he does not, out he goes. Competition is too strong and too widespread to allow him to 'manage somehow' from some hidden sanctuary. So, it is essential for the manager to know how to actualize, maintain and increase his power; and how best he can use it.

The Illusion of Power

A great deal is talked and written about power. Most people think they know what it is; few seem to appreciate its real nature; its origin; its extent; its limitations; its treachery; its illusion. Of special interest is the exercise of a power conferred by reason of status, before any attributes of personality have had the opportunity to show through.

When I first went into general management, I was very impressed by all the powers I was given: what a lot I could achieve with them. I was also somewhat overawed: would I really be sufficiently bold to use them? The facts turned out very different. My freedom to act, merely to attain the objectives laid down, was heavily circumscribed by the rules and regulations emanating from the centre; and, disconcertingly, not only by those, old and new which were promulgated and known, but also by the unwritten ones, handed down through the ages, of which I was not even aware and which the others hardly remembered.

One example made me think deeply about the question. Very quickly, on my taking office as general manager, I had instituted bi-annual fashion shows – very modest affairs, the cost of which was held within the meagre discretionary money allocation I had. We opened the shop after trading hours and models and music were provided by our own staff; the actual costs were the extra electricity used and the cube of cheese and glass of wine offered to all those taking part. The events proved highly successful for the morale of the staff, for the customers who enjoyed the home-made flavour and the familiarity of the occasions, and for turnover and profits. I had hidden nothing, giving pride of place to the events, when they occurred, in our weekly journal.

After some three years, when their success had become a well-established tradition in the store, I happened to mention the forthcoming one in my monthly report to the chairman. I was dumbfounded to get a terse note from him by return, telling me to cancel it forthwith and never to have them again, with no explanation. The dictat was with immediate effect and final. I had to write to the invited customers and cancel. The decision was totally incomprehensible. Then, I learnt, through the grapevine, that fashion shows were not the done thing in that organization.

I also found that the restrictions imposed on me from the centre could emanate from any point in the hierarchy, not just the chairman. The most revealing discovery, however, was the number of points in the branch itself which could, and did, frustrate performance: a careless cleaner who did not meticulously pick up the sticky chewing gum people left behind would cause permanent damage to the new carpets which had cost me months of effort to get central funds to buy; a despatch clerk, unwittingly misunderstanding instructions, would break my undertaking to a customer to send his order on a specific time and day; a slapdash department manager who did not fully brief his section manager would leave a rudderless department, when unexpectedly absent; and so on.

I came to realize that I wasn't all that powerful as a general manager. Most of the paper powers I had were just that – mere paper. I had a large responsibility, but no corresponding real power. Responsibility without power seemed to be my lot. I remember that the phrase that used to come to mind, when I felt unjustifiably boxed in, was 'No taxation without representation'. Just as people had rebelled against the unfairness of being taxed without their being represented at the decision-making process, I felt that it wasn't fair to be held responsible for results whilst being deprived of actual power to bring them about.

My experience of course is not unique. Many managers talk of their frustrations, from both high and low, in their attempts to implement the objectives for which they are made responsible, let alone to do things to bring about change. The cautious and fearful elect for the quiet life and resign themselves to accepting the *status quo* and the average performance. The more enterprising and wilful, whilst encountering many obstacles in their way, work at understanding the real situation and enjoy the challenge and the achievement of changing it, fashioning it, from grassroots level up and conversely up–down, to better fit the requirements.

There are some managers who do not like to admit openly to the actual limitations which deflect their plans, preferring to keep a façade of all-powerfulness. They are the macho ones, parading what they have been able to get and to do, despite all constraints. It is only when you get them in an expansive mood, talking 'off the record', that you get to hear of their complaints of how they are stymied at apparently trivial points. These individuals, at least, are aware of the restrictions and can quietly work at ironing them out, before going ahead with their plans.

The most ineffective are those who, endowed with large powers by reason of their appointment, simply assume that actual power automatically flows from their status and position. They have but to say the word, set the grand strategy, for it to be smoothly carried out. This is an unwarranted assumption, giving them the illusion of thinking that they have powers they do not truly possess – a dangerous illusion which invariably leads to the design, large or small, which is bound to fail.

The higher up managers are in the hierarchy, the more important it is for them to know what the actual powers of the business are; where they are exactly located and who those are who wield them. The value of managing 'by wandering about' precisely lies in being brought face to face with the key power-points and power-holders in the organization which will be different, depending upon the various day-to-day situations of the business.

The Different Kinds of Power

Power is one of those ambiguous, omnibus terms, like freedom and equality, which covers a multitude of meanings. However, unlike freedom and equality which are abstract concepts and to which it is a necessary adjunct, power is, to begin with, a very concrete thing and still retains its physical validity.

The force of a hurricane, of an earthquake, of a volcano is physical, visible and measurable. Animals use physical force, for the most part, to secure their territory and to settle their relations within their group and with outside groups.

In human relations too, physical power, aided and abetted by a gun or a bomb, remains an important arbiter of the age-old question of 'Who rules whom?' Women and children, over time, have been and still are, to some extent, cowed into submission by being subjected to physical violence. The ability to inflict injury or take life, through the use of force, is perhaps the most effective form of power. Cicero made the point when he wrote 'Laws are dumb in the midst of arms'; so did Hobbes in his often quoted comment that 'Covenants without the sword are but words and of no strength to secure a man at all.' Mao-Tse-Tung put it even more bluntly when he pronounced that 'Power comes out of the barrel of a gun.' Even in the new era of reciprocal disarmament by the two superpowers, Reagan's slogan of 'trust but verify' harked to the still immutable need to ensure one's protection through a sufficiency of physical means relative to the other.

Force, however, is, of course, not the only form of power. In human relations, power has become a much more sophisticated instrument. In addition to force or in contradistinction to it, it develops into the means of influence and acquires various abstract connotations. Beauty, for example, a different physical attribute, enables its possessors to exercise power over others to get what they desire. There is the power, the self-control of the mountaineer who scales the heights and reaches the summit; the power of the athletes who, having beaten their competitors, go on to beat their own record. Here the physical component of power is still quite substantial. There is the power of the scientist who discovers the new theory; that of the political leaders who alter the political map of their country; the power of the religious zealot who sways multitudes; that of the businessperson who reshapes and renews his organization. Here, the abstract powers of heart and mind, the intellectual and emotional capacities of individuals to influence others and events, come into play.

The notion of power is also used to compare the relative strengths of individuals. A is said to be more powerful than B, when A can get what he wants, or may want, more easily than B, assuming that B has the same desires. This may be due to A's social position or standing in the hierarchy; or his having more money; or because of his greater knowledge and experience; or his age, sex, certain personal characteristics, even physical strength; or a combination of some or all of these factors.

Even the feelings between individuals are explained in terms of power: thus gratitude. If A does a favour to B, it is, so the theory goes, in expectation of a 'return' favour, if not immediately, then at some time in the future. By doing the favour, A is putting B under an obligation, implicitly compelling B to repay later. 'You scratch my back, I'll scratch yours', 'There's never a free lunch' encapsulate this view of gratitude. A stricter analysis goes still further, holding that A's intention does not matter; it is B's perception that determines the equation: B will feel under A's power and will want to liberate himself by repaying with a favour and clearing the debt. Thus, the most altruistic act is construed in terms of domination. Yet, there is some truth in the theory: the more independent individuals are, the less they like to receive help from others, even when they know that it will be given free and without strings.

Power is used to compare the relative strengths of groups; the power of one country relative to another; the power of the media as against that of government; that of consumers to producers; of management to trade unions; and so on, and, in every case, their corollaries.

Power is always relational. Comparisons are implied, even when the statements are categorical. When we say, for example, that an individual or a country is strong and powerful, we mean to say that they are so, relative to other individuals or countries.

The Fundamentals of Power

In human relations, power and influence, its derivative, have acquired a multitude of meanings, from sheer physical force to the subtlest techniques of persuasion and mind bending, with everything in between. Power has been studied since time immemorial: by military commanders, theologians, philosophers, political thinkers, historians, sociologists, psychologists and many other specialists. Yet, there is no consensus as to what it is, not even between those in the same specialism. Most use the concept without analysing it; those who do, finally, resort to defining it according to their own arbitrary notions which invariably do not tally with those of their peers. The concept very quickly becomes rarefied. A great deal of ink flows but the argument, dealing with abstractions or partial aspects of reality, is never resolved.

In looking at the diversity of views on power, two main schools of thought can be extracted: one that explains it as an instinctive urge and the other as a means to ends.

1 *A basic urge.*

The biologists hold that power is the mainspring of all activity. A new-born baby cries and kicks, signs of its being alive. Their early physical movements are instinctive and disconnected. They learn to coordinate them, through exercise and training. Successfully coordinated activity gives the child power; as they learn to do more things for themselves, they become less dependent on their carers. Jurists speak of the 'will for power' being man's most distinguishing feature and laws have to be made to regulate its manifestations between individuals and groups. Others say it is self-love. Hazlitt wrote that 'the love of power is the love of ourselves'.

As a basic urge, power is said to be desired for its own sake. People simply want to be the focus of attention, at the centre of the action. They enjoy the exercise of power, in their individual ways. Some like telling a good story, because they command attention whilst telling it. One power-hungry individual satisfies his appetite by flaunting the visible symbols of power, the Rolls-Royce, the private jet, the country estate; another gratifies it by keeping a low profile, yet getting known in the right circles as the *eminence grise*, the power behind the throne.

2 *Means to ends.*

Other experts hold that this urge is not self-sufficing, that power is not desired for its own sake. They say people strive for power to use as means to ends, to satisfy their desires, to get what they want. When they are telling the good story, they are satisfying their desire for ascendancy, the desire to keep the others under their sway, and not merely satisfying an urge. The good comedian and actor are satisfying this sense of power when they have their audience 'eating out of their hand'; the sales assistants who continue chatting with their colleagues having seen that you are waiting for them to attend to your need, are exercising power over you; the clerks behind their grille, interminably going on with their paper-work and disregarding the queue of customers waiting are showing them 'who rules whom'. They are exercising power in order to dominate, if only for the limited time-span of the transient relation between them and the others.

The two theories have led to much controversy, as they are supposed to lead to different conclusions. The first, holding that the urge can never be satiated, requires institutional regulation to curb and control it. The second leads to *laissez-faire* and self-regulation. Many find the distinction between the two doctrines more illusory than real.

Whatever urges or instincts we have are surely there for a purpose. We eat because we want to satisfy our hunger (basic instinct) and, in so doing, we ensure our survival (objective). The child throwing a stone in the pool is satisfying an urge for activity and is, at the same time, achieving the objective of disturbing the water and looking at the ripples which the act has produced.

Instinct and objective turn out to be very closely intertwined. Desires turn out to be insatiable, new ones being found as soon as existing ones are satisfied. In practice, the *laissez-faire* of the market has to be bounded by some institutional rules and the self-regulation of groups (doctors, lawyers, the City) also requires some governmental intervention.

The essence of power, then, whether to satisfy an instinctive urge or to use as means to ends, is to get one's way. In the transactions entered into of one's free will, as for example that between the actors and their audience, there is no conflict of wants and the parties are happy in their respective roles. In other cases, where one's wants encroach upon those of the others, or are encroached upon by theirs – where there is competition – power becomes one's ability to carry out one's will.

How to Achieve Power

This brief outline of the concept of power, its meanings and its forms provides a pointer to the means of achieving it. Coercing, rewarding, persuading and convincing, each being used singly or in varying combinations with the others, cover the range of possibilities.

1 *Coercing.*

The use of force, of naked power, may not be necessary. It soon becomes cost-ineffective and counter-productive. The lion turns into the fox. Cunning, in its infinite variety, takes over. The powerful individuals or groups today need not have superiority in physical strength or even in money. They write the agenda, thus determining what is, and what is not, discussable; or they mount the astute propaganda campaign which mobilizes public opinion in their favour; or they know how to make contacts in the corridors of power.

Coercion takes many subtle guises. The implanted fear of a rebuke from the admired person will make many acquiesce to a course of action with which they do not wholeheartedly agree. Subordinates in the work-place will not speak their mind and will agree with their boss, for fear of losing a potential promotion.

Coercion, usually taken to mean the power exercised by the stronger over the weaker party, also works the other way round. The power of the weak, of the powerless to frustrate the strong is, excepting by those who have to bear it, greatly underestimated. A baby determines most of the activities of the family; an invalid often exercises power quite ruthlessly over his carers. In a business, a weak management can lead it to its demise; or a weak labour force, willing but insufficiently trained in the skills required, impedes the best-laid plans and prevents their full realization.

2 *Rewarding.*

As against the beating with the stick, the threat of punishment, there is inducement, the promise of a reward, the dangling of the proverbial carrot. Traditionally, this has been seen to be money. Money certainly buys goods and services, but it does not always buy everything or everyone. The old person, who will not sell his crumbling little house, at any price or at any inducement, to the development company which has all the adjoining land, is unbuyable. Others may be extremely wealthy, but ugly and decrepit. No amount of money will buy eternal youth, beauty and health and they will feel inferior to the penniless, handsome young person. The offer of very high reward packages will not induce certain individuals to work in a country or a city or for a company which does not suit them for personal or ideological reasons. Workers go on strike for long periods and suffer much hardship for matters of principle to them.

In contractual relations, such as exist between employer and employee, the reward package is very important. To expect and receive full commitment, the reward package must be seen to be full and fair; and as money is unlikely ever to be the sole motivating criterion, the intangibles of self-esteem and solidarity should always be catered for, directly by the relevant managers.

3 *Persuading.*

Another means of getting people to do what one wants is through persuasion, making them believe that it is exclusively for their own good. Politicians tell the voters they want to be elected to serve the public, not to satisfy any personal desire. The religious guru promises salvation and seeks contributions, avowedly to serve the cause, but is not averse to dipping his hand into the till. Take-over bidders do not mention the profits that will acrrue to them but wax lyrical about the benefit to shareholders and the economic value generally of unbundling businesses. Directors are not looking after their own interests, they claim, but after those of their shareholders and they want to provide employment, help the community, help the country.

Persuading is manipulating, a different method of coercing people to do one's bidding. You cannot fool all of the people all of the time. In the work-place, as indeed elsewhere, the most clever manipulator is still invariably found out.

4 Convincing.

Convincing is also influencing the others to follow one's course of action, but it is based on full openness: declaring one's interest, proving to the other party that the proposed course of action is right and in their interest and remaining willing to be influenced in return. Scientists publish the full details of their experiments, the findings of which are only accepted after their peers have tested them in their own laboratories or refuted them through submission of counter-evidence. Convincing is the most productive method of influencing. It is based on respect for the other, on sharing knowledge and experience, and it assumes a relationship of relative equality. It is also creative.

In practice, we use whatever power we have to get what we want and will change strategies to that most appropriate to achieve our end. Children learn very early on to do effective cost–benefit analyses. They start by using tantrums – coercing; if they find that these don't work for them, they move over to charming their carers into doing what they want – persuading; or they use a bit of both.

Coercing and convincing stand at opposite ends of the continuum. The trend over time has been to move from the primitive forms of coercion to the convincing method, but there is still no unanimity of view as to which, either singly or in combination, is likely to be the most effective. Much depends on the situation itself and the parties in it. Convincing, for example, is mainly based on reasoning; where this capacity is not yet fully developed, as with young children, the punishment–reward approach is more productive and, in addition, helps them to develop a sense of responsibility.

The Power of Managers

Follett had studied the subject of power in political science and in philosophy and was able to bring her wider outlook and insights when she came to talk about it to managers. She was amongst the first, if not *the* first, to import the study of power into management teaching.

The sources of a manager's power, she always explained, are two-fold. There is the impersonal power granted to them by the employer, through the act of appointment. This represents their formal authority to act, their right to use specified powers to meet given objectives. It is impersonal because it is attached to the job, to be used by whoever is appointed to do it. The second source is personal to the managers and represents their actual capacity to do the job, made up of their expertise, qualities of leadership, and other attributes. It is personal, because it is specific to the individual and will differ, depending upon the person. With the same nominal power, the same objectives and the same resources, two persons will achieve different results, reflecting the differences in their personal characteristics. Both sources, impersonal and personal, go to make the power of the manager, or of any person appointed to do any one job.

I found this distinction between the impersonal and personal strands of one's total power extremely helpful in my first couple of years in general management. It was a valuable antidote to that depressing condition of 'responsibility without power', when I felt irritatingly hemmed in by some organizational rule which prevented me from doing what needed to be done in the prevailing situation. 'Right' I would say to myself 'my impersonal powers are limited, but no one can limit my personal power. How can I increase my personal power to counterbalance the former? What can I learn about the job, about the market, about the customers, about the staff which would enable me to perform better? How can I increase the personal powers of the members of staff to enable them to do their job better?' The limitations of impersonal power were put to work, to provide the challenge of finding ways and means, within them, of circumventing them. The stoppage of the fashion shows was a blow not only to me but to everyone in the store and a great disappointment to the customers. Very quickly, however, we found an alternative. We thought instead of customers' luncheon parties. I checked; this was acceptable to the centre. These luncheons, although more expensive to run in terms of working time and money, proved invaluable – and were perhaps more effective than the fashion shows would have been, in connecting the customers with the life of the store and reciprocally, in making us connect more closely with the local community.

The way managers use the two elements of their power, how much of one and how much of the other and how they combine them in different situations depends upon a complex of factors. To begin with, there is the individual's own temperament. Are they the autocratic or democratic type? Then, there is the task itself. Do they have the full expertise required? Is the task straightforward and essentially repetitive, or complex and subject to continuing uncertainty? What are the resources at their disposal, in terms of people and money? Finally, there is the environment. What is the culture of the company: staid and in-grown or lively and outward-looking? And the outside milieu: stable or volatile? Prosperous or depressed? Of course, nothing is ever either-or. A task, like retailing, is repetitive, but will have the occasional disruption, the emergency, which requires unpremeditated, immediate initiative. A manager may think of men as rational and reliable and treats them as such; of women as emotional and illogical, despite their expertise and qualifications, and treats them, at best, with condescension. The company may be bureaucratic and self-centred but has the nous to employ a few maverick individuals and views their activities with a kindly eye; or be stick-in-the-mud in some functions and innovative in others.

Managers have to understand the intertwining and changing relationships between all these various factors which affect the accomplishment of the task. They have to know themselves and, in particular, understand the nature of the two strands of their power. The difference between the impersonal power of the appointment and the actual ability to do the job is one of kind. The first one gives them the right, the second is their capacity, to do it: two very different things. Of the two, the second is much the more material. The first is, of course, necessary for, without it, they are not entitled to act, but it is not sufficient. The right to do, unbuttressed by capacity to, and willingness to act, becomes very quickly counter-productive.

It is not only the ability to act that is essential, but also, allied with it and equally important, the will to act. To control means to exercise power, to take action, to assume responsibility. This is self-evident but it is surprising how many people think they can have power without accepting the corresponding responsibility. I am still taken aback at meetings, after many years of experiencing it, at the silence that ensues when a question is put and opinions sought. No one is willing to start the ball rolling, each waits for another to make the first move. This unwillingness to declare oneself very often flows into unwillingness to act, into passing the buck, whenever possible.

If a manager has both the authority and the ability to act and yet does not act, it is obvious that he is renouncing control for practical purposes. At best, he will be ignored. The informal organization which grows alongside the formal structure of the company reflects the self-inflicted powerlessness of those nominally in charge. For action, appeal is always made to the persons who can and are willing to do what is required, irrespective of their place in the hierarchy and whether they have the right, or not, to do it.

As against the managers who complain that they have responsibility without power, there are those who want power without responsibility. They cannot have it but, at the same time, they clog the works and damage the smooth running of operations. To achieve power, one must assume its commensurate responsibility. Without such acceptance, power is self-defeating. I experienced some years ago an example of power unused and therefore misused.

I was attached for a short time in a voluntary capacity to the social services department of a London borough to assist the director. One day, a panic message was received in the office: 'The ambulance drivers have come out on strike.' I asked the director what he was going to do about it. 'Nothing' he said 'absolutely nothing. The union is involved; this is a matter for the personnel department. We must not interfere.'

I thought of the long drawn out wrangle which was likely to follow, while the poor out-patients were left standing. I decided, protocol notwithstanding, to find out what the trouble was about. I went down to the MT yard and confronted the ambulance men.

I found a most amenable group of people. To begin with, they were quite amazed that 'someone from up there' had come down to talk directly with them. They had a grievance, of course. It was simple. Many of the out-patients were old and vague and quite incapable of keeping to the programmed pick-up times. The drivers had pointed out the difficulties, both verbally and in writing, but no one had done anything about them. The patients who kept time were made to wait for long periods. They had complained to the supervisor. The supervisor took it out on the drivers. And the shop steward brought the angry drivers out on a lightning strike.

A few soothing words all round and a promise that the social services department would put in a little more organization into helping the geriatrics in the matter of time keeping and the situation was defused. The men went back that afternoon. This occurrence, which could have blown up into a protracted fight, was a classic example of unwillingness to use one's power. The director, although he had the power to initiate action, was unwilling to do so; he preferred to let things ride and then pass the buck to the personnel department.

Many managers expend much energy and ingenuity at politicking to increase their impersonal powers, to get promoted. They could use this energy much more productively to develop their own personal powers, for this is the best means of achieving continuing success. Over time, the right to do goes to those who can and actually do.

There is, as yet, another substantial source of power available to the managers and that is the powers of the individuals in their team. The manager's job is to organize these capacities for best accomplishment of the task. Whether these are used for, or against, depends on how the manager uses his own power in controlling the team members' activities.

By dint of long and painstaking observation of real-life situations and their rigorous analysis, Follett came up with a concept which is of substantial value to managers in getting them to move in the right direction. She developed the concept of power-with as against that of power-over.

Power-over and Power sharing

Almost invariably, when we think of power and how to use it, we think about the power or influence we can exercise over the others or which they can impose on us. The basic premise is of opposing, antagonistic sides. In the business world, management and labour are often against each other. For management, it becomes a matter of having supervisors to ensure that the work gets done well but each supervisory level requires its own supervision and the company soon becomes over-managed with a large supervisory system. This is expensive to run and is not, in any case, all that successful, with the managed finding ways and means to buck the system. Establishing relations on the basis of 'over' and 'under' others does not produce good work.

Through actual experience, we learn that power-over is counter-productive. The trend is to move to the idea of power sharing. We say today that the effective leaders share their power with their people. This is what most forward-looking management theorists enjoin managers to do. Follett thought otherwise. She came to the conclusion that, in reality, we cannot share or delegate or transfer genuine power, that is, the personal power of the individuals, their capacity to act which inheres in them. Their power resides in their experience, knowledge, personal characteristics of heart, mind and character which are specific to them. They cannot detach them from themselves to give to the others. They can, of course, pass on to their subordinates impersonal power, the official authority to act, and also the resources at their disposal, so that the subordinates use them as best they can. But, if they do not know how to use them, the transfer will not only be ineffective in terms of results but can also be destructive.

The alternative to power-over is not power sharing. Sharing or giving power away sounds very nice as a notion, an enlightened act of cooperation. Follett, the meticulous realist, saw that in real life it does not work; indeed that it could not work:

I do not think that power can be delegated because I believe that genuine power is capacity. To confer power on the workers may be an empty gesture. The main problem is, by no means, how much control they can wrest from capital or management . . . This would be a mere nominal authority and would slip quickly from their grasp. Their problem is how much power they can themselves grow. The matter of workers' control, which is so often thought as a matter of how much the managers will be willing to give up, is really as much a matter for the workers: how much they will be able to assume. Where the managers come in is that they should give the workers a chance to grow capacity or power for themselves.[1]

The last two sentences are significant. It is not a question of managers giving any of their powers away. It is one of helping the managed to develop their own and it requires the managed to be willing to assume power, that is, to assume responsibility. We look at this later in this chapter, but first let us look at the power-with concept.

Power-with

If power sharing is not the alternative to power-over, what is? Quite simply, power-with, said Follett. In power sharing, the idea is for managers to share their power with their workers, all going one way, from managers to workers; in power-with, the notion is of joining powers, of both managers and workers pooling their respective powers into the common pot, the current going both ways.

It is a pity and a waste, Follett thought, that the power-with concept was disregarded and almost unknown, for it is also a 'natural'. The person with green fingers is working *with* the plant, freeing it from weeds and bugs, giving it the necessary nutrients and the right soil to enable it to grow to its *own* best strength and beauty. The individual achieves his best integration by organizing his various sub-systems so that each is contributing its due, in coordination with the others, without any one of them being repressed or allowed to take over. The company achieves most by combining the powers of its individual members and by ensuring that its various functions work hand in hand, in unison.

Any function in the company which is given pride of place at the expense of the others, thus allowing it to determine their purpose, sooner or later gets its own come-uppance. This is inevitable, for the supremacy of any one function subordinates the contributions of the others to it, distorting and reducing overall performance. The result is that disillusionment sets in and the once-supreme function is sent to the bottom of the pile, for another one to take over for the time being. Once, it was production, then finance, then marketing that ruled the roost. Currently, it is design which is all-supreme. Design is of course a very important part of the production process, a part which in some areas has not been given its deserved rating. But it is a mistaken enthusiasm which would now subordinate everything to it. Who wants designer chairs one can't sit on, designer clothes one can't walk in, designer gadgetry one can't use, designer shops one can't shop in? Certainly a small international clique of people and perhaps a few museums; exclusive niche marketing can cater for them; but concentrating exclusively on design and disregarding almost completely the functionalism of the item – that it be fit for the purpose for which it is intended – simply does not make sense. Based on the power-over principle, of one function above all the others, it cannot succeed.

Power-with, between individuals, between functions, between interests, is wholly different from power-over or power sharing. It stems from the pooling of powers. By pooling, no one is giving any of his own away. When a car breaks down, its driver is not able alone to move it to the kerb. A helpful person comes along, adds his weight to the driver's and the car is on the kerb in a couple of minutes. There has been no sharing of powers. The separate powers of the two persons have been pooled together to create the joint power which moves the car. Pooling increases total power. By pooling powers, we get not only the addition of the separate powers but also something extra, the extra value created through their joint interaction.

In power sharing, power is accepted as a finite quantity, so that if managers share their powers with their workers they have to lose those parts they are giving to them. The accretion of power to one party is at the cost of the loss of that power to the other party. Some people in the UK, and many eminent ones amongst them, hold that having workers' representatives in the boardroom, as is the case in West Germany, would mean their usurping power from rightful directorial hands. This is based on the premise of having antagonistic sides. This may be the present reality. But it need not always be so. Workers, who are helped to develop their capacities and who themselves evolve their own views, have, and would have, much to contribute in the boardroom, by way of their intimate knowledge of what is and what is not feasible on the shop floor; and their down-to-earth approach would not come amiss in debunking the flights of fancy of some directorial grand strategies.

People do not like giving up any of the power they have. As it turns out, they cannot give it away in any case, and it cannot be taken away from them. If we look at power as 'doing', as 'bringing about change' – and it is these things or it is nothing – it becomes clear that it is not a commodity like a lump of meat that can be divided and distributed, a sum of money that can be taken away from us or which we can give away. Any individual can be prevented, by force, for example, from exercising his power; or his authority to use it can be removed, by ending his appointment, but his own power to do always remains and stays with him. No force or authority can take it away from him.

Power-with: the Win-win Situation

Power-with, unlike power-over which is coercive and repressive, is co-active. It generates its own productivity, creates its own power, its own dynamic. In the work-place, to the extent that we are working on the power-over principle, whether it be by management over labour force or vice versa, whether by the chief executive over the managers, whether by some managers over others, we are wasting resources. Everything that is repressed and not given an opportunity to be used goes bad. Disgruntled or grudging managers or workers know how to use their powers to put spanners in the works. In the UK, it is generally accepted that the power struggle between managements and unions, now beginning to be accommodated into joint endeavour, caused, to a substantial extent, the country's uncompetitiveness in the market-place.

The full plus-value that flows from joint power is not sufficiently appreciated in most quarters. In the few places where it is and where management is learning to canalize individual powers into the tangible force of joint power, the results are very exciting. Japan started its quality-control circles, way back in 1949. The Japanese scientists and engineers felt that the separation of study and analysis from the work routines in industry was ineffective. They could not possibly investigate all the problems of quality and productivity within a plant. These would best be resolved and much more quickly if the workers themselves could deal with them. The know-how came from Dr Deming, the American professor of statistics, who provided the relevant statistical techniques.

There was nothing new about the techniques which had been used in the USA for more than a hundred years. What was new, in the Japanese case, was the teaching of the techniques to the production workers and giving these workers the authority and the power to influence changes in the organization of work, in order to bring about improvements in quality and productivity. Japan's innovation was to invest heavily in training the work-force so that it could develop its own powers and, at the same time, to give it the opportunity to exercise them. The corollary to the investment in training was of course the willingness of the workers to develop their own capacities and to assume corresponding responsibility.

The Q-C circles are an integral part of Japanese business strategy.

Based on the spreading and pooling of knowledge and the unity of effort by the workers themselves to find the better answer, it has been an important element in the Japanese success. It has enabled them to produce well-designed, functional and reliable goods at competitive prices, desired worldwide. Their celebrated 'just-in-time' method of production, mentioned in a previous chapter, is again an application of the power-with principle where sub-contractors and assemblers join their respective powers and collaborate very closely to bring the more competitive and better product to market.

The Japanese methods have been emulated in the West. There is the task force in which anyone who has a contribution to make, whether he be from management or shop floor is attached, on an ad hoc basis, to solve specific problems. There is the project team where individuals, irrespective of status and chosen for their ability to contribute, are allocated to the project from the start to study, plan and implement it. These initiatives have helped a good deal to improve productivity and product quality.

Both the relevant techniques and the underlying philosophy have to combine to give results; neither will work on its own. Training workers whilst subjecting them to stringent supervision and not giving them the power to use their increased knowledge is futile. Giving workers responsibility without giving them the knowledge that enables them to use it effectively is worse than useless. As Follett put it: 'To confer authority where capacity has not been developed is fatal to both government and business.'[2]

The power-with philosophy cannot be planted in alien soil, in the company culture embedded in the strict separation of functions, in the rigid hierarchical structure, where entrenched interests prevail. To graft it in such an environment is a waste of time. It will quickly wither and die, if it is seen as yet another strategem by one party to exercise influence over the other, to carry out its own ends. What is first needed is the habit of mind that connects and joins individual powers. And the managers, as the leaders, are the ones to implant and develop the new attitude, by using the managing process to fulfil its true purpose of creating the joint power of the team which will get the task done to continuing higher standards of performance.

Making Power Grow

Follett's thesis is clear: the more genuine power there is, in terms of capacity to do, in a team or an organization, the greater is its effective productivity, when individual powers are put to work and channelled into joint power. Although managers cannot give their own power away, they can help others develop and grow their own. Following her general thesis, Follett insisted that this was an imperative of the job.

Managers have to get to know their people, their actual and potential abilities. Using actuals, managers can reorganize subsidiary tasks. This may require a redistribution of jobs; something they are doing now could perhaps be done as well, if not better, by others down the line; jobs of others could be enlarged by making them, for example, their own quality controller; or, if they are very good at their job, they could be used to teach its intricacies to the new members of the team. Looking at potentials, managers should suggest and provide as much as possible, internally or externally, the kind of training that would enable these to be realized.

'Shadowing' is the current, supposedly new, discovery, whereby the promising youngster follows the chief executive or the top manager in almost every step to get the real feel of the job. This is not very different from the old 'sitting by Nelly' idea of watching the expert in order to learn from him, a method discredited not so long ago as being old hat and wasteful. Whilst one must be aware of the pitfalls of 'shadowing' (dubious tricks and habits can be learnt from top mentors and the 'shadows' must always retain the critical and questioning attitude), it could with advantage be applied from the top down, so that the top people, sitting by Sid at the machine could learn something from him and he, by teaching, learn something of their ways of thinking and doing.

Not everybody wants power and its concomitant responsibility. Some are bored out of their wits and their prime need is for a challenge to exercise their skills, existing or potential. Others, on the other hand, have outside interests which engage most of their energy and satisfy their need for self-expression; all they want at work is humdrum routine; they would shun extra responsibility. A manager should remember that individuals are unique and have their own scale of values and preferences which they have to respect. We can speculate on the factors involved in motivation, carry out experiments and arrive at findings which are statistically incontrovertible and highly valuable. We cannot, however, automatically, apply them to specific individuals: to find out what makes A and B tick, we have to interact directly with them.

The potential ability which has been developed by training has to be practised, to turn it into an integral part of the individual. Practice turns the training into experience. Once they have acquired the new skill, and applying it well is becoming a habit, they must be given the responsibility and the formal power to go with it. Then, there is the reward element which, as mentioned earlier, has to combine tangibles and intangibles, money and recognition.

Helping the members of the team to develop their own powers is a process which operates to the manager's own advantage and development. If the others in the team can take over parts of the manager's job, they are releasing the leader to look wider and further, to find the bigger challenge, the higher endeavour. Taken to its ultimate, this should result in managers working themselves out of their jobs and qualifying themselves for, and getting, bigger ones.

I was talking to a group of managers on this subject not so long ago. I was intrigued to find that with one of them this was precisely what had happened. As a manager, he had been a conscientious teacher and, as a result, he bitterly reflected, his subordinate had been promoted to his post and he had been made redundant. When I asked him what he was now doing, he said 'Oh, I've now got a better job.' He had actually succeeded on both points, although he had not appreciated the former or expected the latter.

The leader's purpose in training his people is not so that he can sit back, relax and enjoy the fruit of their labour. Quite the contrary: the leader has to work all the harder to keep himself ahead of those he is bringing forward. The work of the leader is not for the faint-hearted. But to empower people to develop their potentialities and become doers in their own right, use them as long as they want to be used and release them when they want to leave to do their own thing is one of the achievements of true leadership; it is also one of its pleasures, almost an indulgence.

Notes

1 Mary Parker Follett, *Dynamic Administration: the Collected Papers of Mary Parker Follett*, Elliott M. Fox and L. Urwick, eds, Pitman Publishing, London, 1973, p. 80.
2 Follett, *Dynamic Administration*, p. 82.

6

Leading and Following: Securing the Future

There are few, if any, organized groups which can achieve their purpose without formal, or informal, leadership. The Society of Friends (the Quakers) appears to have done so. Their members find no need for a minister to preside over their meetings, each being guided to the common goal by his own 'inner light'. However, when individual Quakers embarked on a business enterprise, they did not transfer their 'inner light' principle to it. They provided it with the leadership and the management skills required to ensure a most successful outcome – witness the banking families of East Anglia, the Frys, the Cadburys, the Rowntrees. They knew that a leaderless business was a non-starter.

The fact is that, in the vast majority of organized groups, the principle of leadership is specifically provided for, or tacitly accepted. In one way or another, a leader will emerge. It is as true of the jungle – except for the monkeys, if Kipling's *Jungle Books* are to be believed – as it is true of the nation state and all groups in between. Communes which proscribe the leader's function quickly disintegrate and fail. Cooperatives which survive and succeed do so in direct proportion to their readiness to accept the necessity for leadership and incorporate it in their organization. There can be no group, no team without a leader. Follett saw it clearly:

The leader makes the team. This is pre-eminently the leadership quality – the ability to organise all the forces there are in an enterprise and make them serve a common purpose.[1]

And that really sums it up.

Leading Versus Managing

Leadership is, of course, no new phenomenon in business. What is new is its current hype. It was demoted, after the Second World War, not being fully consonant with the then prevailing view of freedom of letting individuals do their own very thing. It has been rethroned relatively recently. A researcher, surveying the field in the USA in 1985, counted some eight thousand research studies and monographs on the subject and tabulated three hundred and fifty definitions of the term. There are now in the USA no fewer than fifty professors of leadership studies.

The fashionable view now is that leaders belong to a different breed, are a race apart. Managers are out, leaders are in. The management guru will assert that 'what industry needs now is to be led, not managed', or that 'people don't want to be managed; they want to be led'.

In their book, *Leaders: The Strategies for Taking Charge*, published in 1985, Warren Bennis and Burt Nanus create a distinction between leader and manager: 'There is a profound difference between management and leadership . . . The distinction is crucial.'[2] The difference, they say, is between effectiveness and efficiency, activities of vision and judgement versus activities of mastering routines: 'Managers are people who do things right and leaders are people who do the right thing.'[3] They make it sound as though they have unearthed a profound truth.

Their aphorism is certainly a catchy phrase and given their eminence in the field is, unfortunately, by way of becoming the received wisdom. On sober reflection however it simply does not hold up. It was probably Goethe, the universal man *par excellence*, who first said that genius was 95 per cent perspiration and 5 per cent inspiration. Efficiency and effectiveness are the inseparable foundations of any successful activity, whether it be the activity of the poet endlessly searching for the right words to express his vision, or that of the scientist testing the validity of his hypothesis in the laboratory, or that of the businessperson making sure that the organization actually has the resources to carry out his grand design.

Any activity is ineffective to the extent that it is inefficiently carried out. Companies get taken over not only because of lack of vision but, equally as often, because of the surfeit of vision of their leaders, not backed by mastery of routines. The history of business is littered with examples of visionaries who failed, because of their ignorance or neglect of the routines. The Japanese started as copiers of other people's products, being, according to the distinction made by Bennis and Nanus, merely efficient. This did not prevent them from becoming most effective in the market-place and, in due course, themselves creating products which others now want to copy. They do the right thing because they do things right and they do things right because they do the right thing.

The view that crowns the leader as a 'supremo', the one who provides the inspiration, the judgement and the charisma, and the managers, as the people who simply master the routines, is essentially divisive and out of date. It is harking back to the days of the dichotomy between 'thinking' and 'doing'; except that no longer is the division between the 'manager' and the 'hands', but between the 'leader' and the mere 'managers'. Practising managers know that leading and managing are inseparable aspects of the same task and that the distinction is, as some of them have put it, 'a lot of bunk'. I found, in my experience, that some of the most original and worthwhile ideas came from individuals on the shop floor and that they could be implemented because they arose out of an intimate knowledge of the facts; most of mine, which I thought brilliant, came to nought, because there was no way of connecting them with what was in place and could not be changed.

To separate leading and managing, to say as Bennis and Nanus do, that 'what's needed is not *management* education but *leadership* education' is probably meant more as a thought-provoking antithesis than a serious suggestion that the management function can, or should be, separated from the obligation to lead. But it can cause confusion and any attempt to translate it into action would be likely to result in poor performance all round. The leader who is not a manager turns out to be flawed and so does the manager who is not a leader.

Certainly there are managers without the real qualities of leadership. They are just poor managers. In fairness to Bennis and Nanus, it should be said that much of their book is devoted to disproving the either/or thesis they have formulated in favour of the combined double-function conviction. But they have coined a catch-phrase which will for some time influence attitudes and behaviour in some ways. This is both regressive and damaging.

A Personal Essay in Leadership

My early life and professional training had never led me to expect to become a manager. Yet at the age of 40, and entirely without experience, I found myself the general manager of a department store with a staff of some four hundred people. The store was in a run-down state, staff morale was low and a general air of lethargy prevailed. I knew at once that I had to revitalize the place and that the way to start was with the staff.

Fortunately, there was a good in-house communication system. I took advantage of it. At meetings with the rank and file, I told them what I felt most sincerely: that each job, however menial it appeared, was essential to the well-being of the store and no less important than mine. Without their specific contributions, the shop could not operate successfully. There was not much point in having exciting merchandise to sell, if customers were put off by indifferent or careless service in any of their dealings with the store, whether with the accounts clerk, the telephonist, the despatch clerk or the selling assistant. High personal standards of conduct were the essence of professionalism and each one owed it to his self-respect, his self-regard, to be professional. To serve did not mean to be subservient. Our customers needed us as much as we needed them. And I certainly needed every bit of individual help the staff could give me; I was new to retailing, knew nothing about it and was relying on them to teach me its mysteries. I hoped that my specialism, accountancy, would be of help in taking the store onwards and forwards.

The picture that had developed in my mind's eye was of the shop as our day-time home, and this is the way I put it to them, that it was *our* shop, *our* day-time home and each and every one of our customers was a welcome and honoured guest. One's responsibility to please did not, however, exclude one's own personal enjoyment. When we had guests at home, we, as the hosts, also enjoyed the occasion. Our motto was to be twin-pronged: 'Shopping at . . . is Fun. Working at . . . is Fun.' This theme of taking up and enjoying personal responsibility was also emphasized at meetings with staff and line managers. And, to start off on our new relationships and our new life together, we would have a spring-clean throughout the store, with a competition and prizes going to the selling and non-selling departments, assessed highest on cleanliness. The shop soon looked sparkling and lively, and so did the staff.

Having started to tackle the internal situation, I had to look outwards. We needed to build our clientele. We had no advertising budget, central policy being against advertising. I sought ideas from the staff. The idea of the fashion show mentioned in chapter 5 had in fact come at a rank and file meeting from a young, Saturday-only selling assistant. When I pointed out that we had no experience for such an event and that we would be very amateurish, an accounts clerk chimed in with 'Why don't we call it a *home-made* fashion show?. Our customers will understand.' This is indeed how we put it in our invitations to them. And it was very much that *home-made* element which gave the shows their charm and their value. It somehow created a bond between the customers and us: all the little disasters which occurred or were successfully avoided during the shows became links to start a chat or a buying transaction, the customer for example telling the selling assistant 'Do you remember that time I stopped you just in time from falling over?'

Various other innovations were introduced, many at the suggestions of the staff. The fashion shows had to be abandoned, by edict. So, we started customers' luncheon parties, at which I would invite members of staff, irrespective of status, but required because of their knowledge about some item on the agenda.

The first such luncheon produced a totally unexpected result. The first item I had put down on the agenda was 'How can we improve our service to you as customers?', put down with much trepidation, anticipating their complaints of our being invariably out of stock of the very item they wanted. Their need turned out to be very different and very basic. 'Could we please have an extra loo in the cloakroom? The shop being so much busier now, this is necessary.' The service manager was called in and brought the plans of the cloakroom area; the rest of the agenda was forgotten about and we set to finding out whether it could be done and 'yes, it could be done'. And the extra loo was soon provided.

At another luncheon party, one of the subjects I had put down for discussion was 'How can we be of use to the community?' This brought an idea, from a customer who was a member of the WVS, that perhaps we could open the shop one evening in the Christmas period to allow long-term patients at nearby hospitals and homes to personally do their own Christmas shopping. The idea was put to the staff and they welcomed it wholeheartedly. This became a joint community effort. The Rotarians made themselves responsible for the transport; the WVS and other voluntary women's bodies offered to accompany the patients; the police kept the street space free for the ambulances; and the staff stayed, at no extra pay, to serve these very special people, bringing their own home-made mince pies to accompany the tea we were offering. This proved a great event indeed. It was to become a regular feature in the store's calendar.

The achievement here was not the profit – the actual spend by these customers was very small and the profit on it insufficient even to cover the extra costs involved in keeping the store open. The achievement was of course the unity of purpose joining all those involved, and actualizing itself in the occasion: seeing the happy and eager faces of the handicapped guests in their wheel-chairs, who had not been in a shop for perhaps many years, marvelling at the sparkling store bedecked with Christmas merchandise and working out very carefully what their funds would run to buying. As I write this, the picture of that first Christmas Shopping Evening some twenty-five years ago returns brilliantly to mind, and especially its tangible feeling of good fellowship.

The customers became our best intelligence; it was their store too and they wanted us to succeed. They would come and tell me that our competitor was selling something we were not stocking and wasn't this a pity? I had told them of that bugbear of the chewing gum, and I saw them very often picking it up from the carpet themselves. In small and large ways, they too became part of the life of the store. One of them saved me from what would have been a most embarrassing situation.

It was the habit of the organization to invite its customers to musical evenings. (Fashion shows, frivolous and too near the trading bone, were *infra dig*, but musical evenings, serious and decorous, were part of its traditions.) This was organized by the centre and a quintet with a world-famous violinist had been booked for our occasion. The invitations had been sent out and, then, just a fortnight before the event, I received a telephone call from the local booking officer: as a customer, he had received the invitation but the venue could surely not be right. The local Guildhall was already booked for that evening, and not by us. Alarm bells rang. There had been a breakdown in communication: the person at the centre had thought that I would book the hall this time and I had thought the whole thing would be organized by him. But the bookings officer continued his rescue work. He found us an alternative venue; new invitations were urgently despatched. The evening was a great success. But a disaster it would have been, were it not for that thoughtful and well-disposed customer who alerted me to the mistake and then went out of his way to help in putting it right. It was the fund of goodwill that the store had created in the town actualizing itself in the assistance of this customer that saved that situation.

In the shop itself, the activities we generated created their own dynamic; each new idea tried and implemented led to something else. All this purposeful activity gave new life to the staff. They developed as a team, with individuals becoming conscious of their worth and wanting to make their mark. Friendly rivalry and competition flourished. Which department had the highest sales? Which the smallest number of complaints? Which individual had been commended for initiative? Which driver had been able to fathom out an incomplete address and get it right first time? And so on.

In no time at all, it seemed, there was a metamorphosis of the store. Profits mounted and the staff bonuses in parallel. From being the Cinderella in the chain, it became a leader. The other heads of branches began to scrutinize our weekly journal to see which ideas they could borrow. The change in the store became the talk of the town, an unpaid advertisement.

It wasn't of course all sweetness and light. There was shoplifting by customers and staff. There was politicking between managers. There were crises. There were those for whom the new regime was too much like hard work. Trade had its downs. There were troubles and conflicts with the centre. But the underlying thrust remained always 'forward, with gusto and with feeling'.

The question that still exercises me is: 'How come that I turned out an effective manager and leader?' I had had no management education, no leadership education. I had been an accountant, with a degree in economics. My previous work had been in the international field, involved in feasibility studies for capital projects in countries in South America and Eastern Europe. Retailing and its ethos were totally alien to me. My shopping was strictly limited: for clothes, Aquascutum at sale time and Marks & Spencer at other times; replenishments for the home were few and far between; I seldom went into department stores which were in any case then too fiddly for me.

What I did, and this is before I had discovered Follett, was to respond naturally to the situation; the apathy and the listlessness of the staff just did not feel right. In wanting the people in the shop to be alive and kicking, I simply wanted to bring this about for its own sake. I was not working out how much this would mean to bottom-line profits – not that I, as an accountant, was unaware of the importance of these.

Could it be that women, especially if untainted by too much management, leadership or ethical education of the kind available in business schools worldwide, and thinking things through for themselves, naturally make effective managers and leaders? I think this could be the case.

I was doing well, but I wanted to do better. Doing things that came naturally or instinctively was not good enough. I wanted to learn what the professionals had to teach about managing, a long quest that culminated in my discovering Follett and her philosophy. Quite by chance, I had not been so very far from her teachings. She wrote of the leader as the man who can energize his group, who knows how to encourage initiative, how to draw from all what each had to give. Although I was a woman, I had been able, it seemed, to do something like that.

The Function of the Leader

The function of the leader, whether the chief executive running the large global enterprise or the obscure manager very much down the line with one or two staff is, whilst differing in scope, essentially the same. Follett summarized it as 'group accomplishment on a continuing basis'. This comprises defining the common purpose, determining the mode of association, building the future, sharing experience and turning the followers into leaders.

1 *Defining the common purpose of the task.*

To operate effectively, people need to know their place in the scheme of things and their contribution, present and potential, to it. Without such positioning, they become alienated, subject to that anomie which Durkheim found to be the debilitating malady of industrial society and still with us today, in our so-called post-industrial age. Just as the successful business positions itself and achieves best when it finds its niche in the market, so individual workers are likely to perform best when they know their place in the business; and just as the company's niche in the market is not fixed forever but is changed to create opportunity and growth, so the individuals' places in the enterprise are not fixed points but ones that they can move forward, as they adjust their contribution to its evolving needs, and grow with it.

To define purpose is to clarify it in its myriad ramifications. Why are we producing this particular piece of equipment, selling this service? Why do we need good work? Why profit? Why do we have to do better than our competitors in meeting customers' needs and wants? Why must we meet shareholders' expectations of a satisfactory return? Why the need to take the long view? Why the interdependence of interests? And it is not only the whys, but also the whos, the hows and the whats that have to be explained. Who are our customers, our competitors? How are we going to satisfy the one and surpass the other? How can we improve our standards? What are our objectives for this year, next year and the year after? And so on.

It falls to the chief executive, as the overall head and leader of the whole enterprise, to synthesize the answers to the questions into the general purpose that energizes the people, that gets them going to do things right and to do the right thing. It falls to the managers, however small their group may be, to do the same in specific detail for the members of their team, always remembering and emphasizing that purpose is not a static given thing, but is always evolving, a purpose which the members are themselves shaping and fashioning by the very work they are putting into it.

The more complex the business, the more convoluted the strategy, the greater is the need to explain and make it accessible to those who, in however small a way, have to carry it out. The leader is the one who has the power to make purpose manifest, who is able to talk to his co-workers in the language they understand and can make them see that it is not his purpose which is to be achieved, but the common purpose growing out of their own activities. The co-workers are put in the picture, the overall picture, seeing their specific positions in it, enabling each in this way to see his place in it better, to connect better with the others and therefore to contribute individually that more effectively. The leader brings the purpose home to them, stimulates them to give what they can to it and, in the process, helps them to make it their very own.

2 *Determining the mode of association.*

With the purpose clearly explained and shared, the mode of association has to be resolved. The question 'On what basis are we going to work together?' has to be clearly answered by the leader. Is it to be on the strict division of activities and truncated responsibilities, the command–obedience method, or it is to be team-work with joint and collective responsibility, the cooperating method? Given the whole tenor of this book, it is evident that the second method is considered the more effective, for both the business and the individuals in it.

There are many variables to be considered. The tasks themselves and the technology available have to be taken into account, but these are subsidiary to the people themselves. Tasks can be arranged for either centralized or decentralized decision making, the technology being available to make either feasible. First and foremost, however, it is the people involved in the task that have to be studied.

Do they want freedom of action with its corollary of personal responsibility and closer interlinkings with the others? Are they sufficiently knowledgeable and experienced to make the appropriate judgement and the right decision without specific direction? Or sufficiently sure of themselves to know when to make the decision, and when to seek advice? If they are, well and good; the leader can set up the organization structure – flatter, with a smaller number of supervisory levels, with power spread to the peripheries and with the proper interlinkings – that goes with the cooperating method. If they are not, if they are used to authoritarian leadership and to passive following of orders, the leader has first to change their attitudes, to train them in the new ways and to convince them, by example, that the new method is of as much benefit to them as it is to the business.

This is extremely important. Many companies, heady with the scent of success which participative management augured, went in for major organizational restructuring to put it in place, only to find that it did not work. They had not trained the managers and, through them, the work-force to operate in the different framework. The people were either mistrustful of the new-fangled arrangements or did not know how to behave within them.

The structure of the organization determines the means of communication connecting tasks and people. The mode of association is the code of behaviour that manager and managed evolve between themselves to get the job done. It is, to be sure, largely determined by the structure in place and by the culture of the company, but it is not exclusively so. Managers, within their own enclave, are free to change the mode of association with their people. A new code, however, cannot be simply imposed. It has to be tried and tested, seeded and grown. As always, the managers as the leaders are the initiators of change. They lead by example. Through building the self-confidence of the members in the team, through sharing knowledge with them, getting them to develop their own points of view and using what is valuable in them to arrive at decisions, through building mutual trust and in innumerable other ways, the managers prepare the ground on which the cooperating method can take root and blossom.

I remember one small thing in my early days which came perhaps more by accident than by design. As a residue of my old French education, I do not feel comfortable using Christian names, except with family and very close friends. In the store, there was some hierarchical rule, whereby the rank and file were called by their Christian names. Combined with that dislike of using Christian names was my feeling that it was not right to call subordinates, much my seniors in years, by their Christian name whilst they had to address me by my surname. So, I called everyone in the store by their surname. The department managers, in talking to me about members of their staff, had to refer to them by their surnames, as I would not have known who they were talking about otherwise. Somehow, being referred to by surname made the rank and file feel elevated in status; somehow, they grew in their own eyes in stature and self-confidence.

Changing the form does not by itself change the mode of relating with one another. The manager may declare an open-door policy but nothing is changed if subordinates who walk through that open door, are sat down, made to listen to a short or long monologue and then sent out without having had the opportunity to make themselves heard. Managers would do much better to keep their door closed until they have learnt how to listen. It is said that the single greatest attribute of the effective leader is being a good listener.

3 Building the future.

Anticipating tomorrow's task is as important as carrying out today's. Successful leaders see in their mind's eye the new situation before it becomes actuality. They see the picture arising out of the current position, the things which belong to the present picture but which are not yet painted into it and those things that have to be removed from it. Their insight becomes foresight which enables them to take the decisions today which are laying the foundations for tomorrow's situation. In this way, they are creating in part the incoming situation and thus, in a very real sense, controlling the future.

In all of these activities, the managers have to include the members of their group. Unless they do this, unless each member has had a say and a part according to his ability in the making of that picture, the group is unlikely to be at its most potent. There can be no realism and no logic in expecting full commitment if there is no involvement in the first instance.

Foresight may be the last gift of the gods to mortals but one can prepare oneself to receive it. Having got bored once with a central buyer and justifications based 'on hindsight', I told him more in jest than in earnest: 'How about making your foresight as good as your hindsight?' This seemed to work. He thought ahead a little more carefully, envisaged likely happenings and built into his buying greater flexibility to meet possible contingencies. Indeed, so successful was he that the other buyers adopted the injunction as their own. 'Make your foresight as good as your hindsight' became the slogan of that buying office.

Foresight comes from curiosity, from a clear head wanting to understand why certain things happened in their complex ramifications, organizing that experience to deduce what would be likely to happen in the future in the context of different configurations of circumstances – the most likely scenarios – and taking appropriate steps to change, or compensate for, the negative factors and capitalize on the opportunities. Foresight is a function of both intelligence and character. A timorous, fearful person will interpret the facts differently from the energetic, optimistic individual of equal intelligence and will plan differently for the future. It is the right fusion of intelligence and character that goes to make effective foresight. Luck, good or bad or a bit of each, will affect the best-laid plans. This is an intrinsic part of the business of doing. We have always to leave something – not too much – to chance.

The effective leader, in foresight as in everything else, leads by example. By showing his co-workers how he organizes his experience (how he analyses past and existing situations, projects them into the future and envisions the likely scenarios to come) and, flowing from this, the decision the leader takes today to shape tomorrow's future to advantage, helping co-workers to develop their own curiosity and their own will to better anticipate and create their own future.

4 *Sharing experience.*

In chapter 3, in discussing the managing process, the importance of manager and managed developing a common field of experience was highlighted. It seems that we cannot transfer experience to others. Rare are the people who can learn from the experience of others. We have to go through the actual experience of doing to find out what it means. It is only then that the experience of the others acquires relevance for us. The poet and the painter illuminate and enrich our experience. They cannot serve it to us by proxy.

Thus, it is not sufficient for the leader to explain and involve – just in words. The involvement has to be concretized in action, through leader and followers doing things together and also through the followers working together. A lasting agreement between them can only come through their sharing each other's experience. The leader, through the cooperating mode of association, creates the conditions which permit this mutuality. It takes longer to arrive at decisions but this, Follett said, is not time wasted. The sharing of views and experience has value 'as a way of taking our co-workers along with us step by step in the acquiring of information, in comparing that information with past experience, in the whole process by which judgements are reached and decisions made'.[4]

It seems that the Japanese are past masters in this method of decision making. It takes them a long time to arrive at a decision; the proposal goes back and forth to all those likely to be involved in the task and the decision is only made when most reservations have been cleared and when those who were originally against the proposal have had psychological time to adjust to the evolving consensus. It gives the decision common consent and, once made, the action is rapid and carries the loyal cooperation of all.

It is through the actual doing together, through the common experience that solidarity evolves, that the team spirit becomes a fact. Similarities of views and habits develop; the individuals in the group understand each other, each one knowing how the others think and are likely to behave. In the occasional absence of the leader, the group will continue to function effectively, for its members will have the self-confidence, borne out of the shared experience, to do what is needed. It is also through the doing together that mutual control grows, the kind of control that becomes self-control.

5 *Turning his followers into leaders.*

Perhaps the most exciting element of the leader's function is to train his followers to become leaders in their own right. As we saw in the previous chapter, he cannot give them his own power but he can help them to build their own. The leader knows that his job is not to make the decisions for the subordinates, neither is it blithely to command them to 'go and sort it out'. It is to teach them how to handle problems themselves, how to make their own decisions. The leader gives them responsibility and shows them what is necessary for them to do in order to meet it. 'To persuade men to *follow* you and train men to work *with* you are conceptions of leadership as far apart as the poles'[5] – so Follett was teaching seventy years ago, something that still has to be learnt today.

The best type of leader does not want men who just acknowledge the leader's power and render passive obedience; or those that can be overwhelmed with a strong charismatic personality and who follow because they simply believe in that leader. The leader does not want to be in charge of a lumpen mass, where followers abdicate their own powers of heart and mind and do anything at the leader's bidding. 'The best leader' Follett said 'has no followers but men and women working with him.'[6] Elsewhere, she ringingly proclaims, 'The best leaders train their followers to become leaders . . . The great leader wants to be a leader of leaders.'[7]

Types of Leadership

The three hundred definitions of leadership counted in 1985 in the USA alone have handsomely proliferated since then, and different types of leadership spawn in bewildering confusion. As leadership is indissolubly bound up with power, the leader being the one who has power to get things done, it is much more sensible to simplify the proceedings and categorize leadership types by power source. Follett thus identified three main types: leadership of position, of personality and of function.

Ideally, all three should be in the same individual: the leader should be the one who has the official authority to act, the charismatic personality to inspire and the knowledge and experience relevant to the task in hand. In practice, it is not always possible to get the ideal combination. Follett maintained that the priority for managers, as indeed for any individual, is to develop their functional leadership.

1 *Leadership of position.*

Directors are elected by their shareholders. The other managers of the business have leader-positions by virtue of their appointments. Leaders are elected or appointed because they have *prima facie* the right combination of personal traits and skills to enable them to lead in the positions in which they have been placed. Leadership of position, in principle at least, follows those of personality and function. But this *de jure* right to lead is to begin with nominal only; important as it is because it gives legitimate authority to act, it has to be validated through action. It becomes *de facto* when the leader actually delivers.

This is clearly seen when there is a new person in charge. It is fascinating to watch, at first hand, the workings of the evolving relationship between the new manager and the members of his group. However stable the situation of the department or company, the appointment of a new departmental head or a new chief executive augurs change for the unit. Prior to the arrival, there is anticipation, uncertainty and apprehension. When the new person comes in, there is a period of familiarization, then mutual assessment and finally accommodation.

The subordinates will judge their new chief on whether he has a clear view of the task with which they can agree, and can help them to work more effectively together to achieve it; whether, in fact, the new leader can deliver. If he cannot, his nominal right will be of no avail. The assessment may not be immediate; the subordinates may give him the benefit of the doubt, wait and see how he settles down and develops but the proof of the pudding is always in the eating: is the manager able to deliver?

2 *Leadership of personality.*

To be a good communicator is, of course, very important to the leader. The powers to articulate purpose, to communicate it and to energize people into effective action – these form the charisma of the leader which binds his followers to him. But this attribute without, at the back of it, knowledge and application to the nitty-gritty of detail is insufficient by itself to make the long-distance leader. On their own, the persuasive skills of the leader will work, but not for long.

One chief executive I knew had an extraordinary gift of the gab. He would enthral the whole board and get his policies agreed, only for the directors to realize afterwards, in the cool of their office, that the decisions made were unworkable. He lasted three years. His almost hypnotic influence on people could not hide his deficiencies; the business quickly started going downhill and it took two years to get him out. His powers of persuasion had got him selected and elected and he was rightfully in place to exercise his leadership. But there was no effective capacity to lead, in terms of relating vision to actual resources, behind his eloquent phrasemongering. His failure was inevitable.

We selected a very different type to follow him, a modest man who 'only wanted to learn'. His way was very different. He went through each department spending time with its manager and staff to find out exactly how things worked. In some four months, he had mastered the actual workings of the business in depth. He then started to suggest ways of improving operations in each department; as they were of real help to manager and staff, they were eagerly implemented. He did the same to the trading policies, looking at what was there, finding out what was good and had to be retained, what could be improved and what had to be discarded. Objectives were similarly treated. It was truly amazing how quickly that man turned the company around, from near extinction to health and strength, quite a little power in the market. And everyone developed the greatest affection, respect and admiration for him.

There is a general tendency to overrate personality, especially these days when 'being good on television' is such an important criterion for success. It is worthwhile bearing in mind, however, that the really great leaders, whether political, military, business or otherwise, have always had, in addition to their charismatic qualities, the skills relevant to their specialism. It is that knowledge and experience that give strength and substance to their personality. Follett instanced Joan of Arc, that leader apparently owing all her power to her voices. 'Her leadership was obviously and pre-eminently due to the ardour of her conviction and her power to make others share that conviction – yet we are told that no trained artillery captain could excel Joan of Arc in the placement of guns.'[8] And Follett's advice to the aspiring leader: 'Forget your personality; learn your job.'

3 *Leadership of function.*

Irrespective of position or personality, true leadership lies in the individual who knows his job, who can grasp the essentials of what needs to be done and also the relational significance of the facts in hand. The machine operator, who knows how its parts interlock and can put them right when something goes wrong in their connections, becomes the magnet which attracts his colleagues, when something goes wrong with theirs. Irrespective of title, that person, Follett maintained, *is* the leader for that specific task. In our every need, we always seek that person who can actually help in the particular predicament in which we find ourselves, irrespective of title or position.

Leadership of function predicates the existence of multiple leaderships and multiple followerships. Given the variety and complexity of requirements in business today, its management cannot be held in one pair or in a few pairs of hands, if it is to prosper. Each member of the groups in it has a particular strength, a specific knowledge, not always determined by official position. Effective leaders seek out these individual abilities to capitalize on them. They put them to work to the common task. They organize the work sufficiently flexibly to allow the person with the knowledge and the technique relevant to the situation to control that situation. And if that situation is likely to be sufficiently permanent, they recognize that person's *de facto* leadership by backing it with official authority to act. That person becomes the leader – whom even the leaders themselves follow – in that particular field of action.

Followers and Followership

Even though the stereotype view of leadership as command-and-obedience is now generally rejected, the view of the led as passive followers lingers on. We still tend to think of the leader as all-important and the rest as not much more than a mass of undifferentiated people, complying at the leader's behest. The leader is the star; the others, at best, consenters. Most attention is concentrated on how leaders can influence their followers and the techniques used to keep them in line; very little attention is paid to studying the role of the followers and how they can, and should, influence and control them. Leaders and leadership are obsessively analysed; followers and followership almost totally ignored. This is a waste, for the followers have as much to give their leaders as they have to them.

To see 'following' as merely an adjunct to 'leading' is to miss the real nature of the group process, the reciprocal influencing going on all the time between leader and led and between the followers themselves. The leader, as we saw when looking at the group process, is of the group, being influenced by the others as he is influencing them. All energy and power do not flow solely from the leader to the led; the current goes all ways: from the leader to them, from them to the leader and also between the led themselves.

Leading and following are complementary functions, the two elements of the same process which materializes in activity. The leader needs his followers as much as they need him. The needs are reciprocally equivalent. Together, they translate into the joint effort which determines the standard of performance of the task. That standard will be higher, the greater the contributions of leader and followers and the better their intermeshing. Followership, properly understood and exercised, is active participation; it cannot yield its full value otherwise. Even at the theatre or at the concert, where the followers are essentially spectators, the players know how much they need their active involvement to be able to give of their best: their acting is itself part-reacting.

Followers should follow not through blind obedience, not even through consent but through self-willed, fully-fledged acceptance. Otherwise, they are not fulfilling their function. It should never be a matter for the followers to leave it to the leader or expert exclusively to pronounce on what needs to be done, on the ground that 'they know best'. This is inert consent, mainly due to laziness, not wanting to be bothered to find out why it is best. Such consent is unproductive, worse than the child's *pro tem.* acceptance of the parental dictat that 'Daddy knows best', only to come back later with continuing questions and learn as a result. The converse of the leader's responsibility to explain the whys and wherefores is mirrored by that of the followers to ask these questions and get answers which they can either accept wholeheartedly or get changed through their own views and insights.

The followers also have knowledge and experience, different from their leader's. They should put these into the pool, personally contributing to reach the most appropriate action. For them to say after the event, as many of them often do, 'We knew all along it wouldn't work; we could have told you this even before you started' is plain irresponsibility. If they have reservations or doubts about the validity of a given lead, they should voice it, so that these can be brought to bear in making it that little bit more accurate, that little bit more appropriate to the situation in hand.

In both cases, by following sheep-like the 'the leader knows best' call or remaining silent when aware that something will not work, the followers are abrogating their responsibility to help the leader arrive at the better decision, that which will result in a more effective performance of the task as a whole. They let their leader down; they also let themselves down. The whole group suffers.

The genuine, cooperative interplay between leader and led and between the managed themselves has to be continuous. No situation remains static, but evolves and changes. The leaders cannot remain in control, if they are not kept cognizant of the facts as they are developing. If their followers keep these away from them, revealing only those they think the leaders would like to hear and not those that ought to be heard, they are again failing in their role as followers, failing their leader, themselves and their group as a whole.

The same reciprocity also applies to accountability. Just as they, the managed, are accountable for their performance and accept their manager's monitoring, so the manager too is accountable to them for his contribution to the common task; and they should make the leader so accountable. Accountability has to work both ways: as the manager keeps them on their toes, so they keep him on his. This is the most effective way the group controls itself. The controls exercised by the shareholders, the market, the bankers, the competitors come after the event and therefore that little bit too late. Those exercised by the followers on the leader, in-house and on an ongoing basis, anticipate the external constraints and, by timely action, circumvent them. The self-control exercised within the group does not dodge the outside controllers; it confronts them full on: by pre-emptive corrective action, it avoids their intervention.

The function of every follower in the group is to be an active participator in it. It is essential for each follower to exercise personal responsibility and take part: to retain individual integrity, to keep the leader in control and to ensure the best success of the group's endeavour. In this way, a group member becomes a true partner or principal, albeit a junior one, not a mere agent, in the action.

Underestimating or underusing the potential of the followers is, *ipso facto*, reducing that of the leader. To view with suspicion any show of independent thought by the followers is a relic of the command-and-obedience indoctrination, still embedded in our thinking. Much will be gained in increasing the total force of the group, when followership will be studied with as much attention and care as that currently given to leadership. Followership has to be valorized at its true worth. That was Follett's constant message.

Developing Followership

My early attempts to energize the staff were based more on intuition than known principles. That they achieved a fair measure of success was evidenced by the performance figures, improved customer and staff relations and the final blessing – official approbation. I should have been satisfied, perhaps. But reading Follett made me understand the function of the manager in greater depth. She made me ask myself: 'Am I doing enough to make my followers active participators in the action?'

Through this questioning, I came up with the idea of a questionnaire for everyone in the store to assess my performance. As I was assessing theirs on a close and continuing basis, why should they not assess mine? Admittedly, my own performance was assessed by my superiors, but what about my own followers? They experienced the ways I managed, day in and day out, and surely they would be the best people to judge the quality of my leadership. By the same token, they could give me leads on how to improve my contribution.

Two friends, a market researcher and a statistician, devised with me a set of 20 questions to be ticked on a 5-point scale from 'excellent' to 'poor'. The idea, when I put it to the various groups in the branch, was received with not a little suspicion and they voiced it 'What are you on about now? Is this to get something on us you can use against us later?' I explained its purpose 'I am telling *you* all the time you can do better. How about a bit of reciprocation and you telling me how *I* can do better?' I was only interested in the overall findings, the individual questionnaires would at no time come into my possession and the three-person committee, to be chosen by them, would destroy the papers, once the analysis was completed.

A month later, I was presented with the findings which were in the main surprising. On both the plus and minus points, they had picked unexpected things. My best point was that I had improved the reputation of the store but, as illustration, they gave not examples of what I had done as a part of my job, but the talks I had given on the history of the store to outside groups.

This had arisen completely by accident. The history of the branch dated back to Napoleonic times; I had become fascinated by it and had studied it in detail; I would give a five- to ten-minute talk on it to the new recruits. A part-time assistant who heard it was a member of the local Historical Society. She mentioned it to its secretary who asked me whether I would talk to the Society. The thing snowballed. Other local associations asked me to talk about the store to their members. One such event had been reported in the paper. Finally the talk itself was printed in it. As a result, everybody in the store became a somebody. Each worked at 'XYZ' – that shop with the exciting history. Thus, something that I had done out of personal interest, completely outside my sphere of official responsibility, had appealed to them most.

One of my worst points was that I was a bad listener. I had heard this before, from my children who always blamed me for being too impatient and not paying real attention to what they were telling me. The other negative was that I was hot-headed and impulsive, making immediate decisions which I would rescind later, after reflection. This did surprise, for I had thought that I left my impulsive self at home and only brought my most rational side to work. I did pride myself on my rationality; but I had to bow to the evidence. I undertook to do my best to mend my ways and to consult more often with the two most senior department managers. In fact, we developed a code. A certain look, a certain smile told me when I was beginning to lose my cool and brought me to heel.

On the whole, I thought this exercise to involve the followership more closely with the leadership paid off. The other heads of branches who read about the survey in our weekly journal did not copy this particular innovation. Some thought it was naive; others commented to me that it sprang from an inferiority complex; yet others said I wanted to be loved. Perhaps so. The fact remains that, for us in the branch, the questionnaire and my acting on it strengthened the bond between us. The managed learned that, as Follett had put it, 'the current had to go both ways'. They had to keep their manager on her toes, as she kept them on theirs.

The fact that I had subjected myself to their scrutiny did not reduce my authority. On the contrary, I found that it increased it. I could now criticize their performance more directly and more openly and, as a result, they knew more exactly what was expected of them. I, in turn, had learned of my weaknesses and worked at reducing them.

This experience demonstrates, I think, what Follett was advocating some seventy years ago. It is not sufficient for the leader to motivate their group; its members, too, have to motivate the leader. It is the leader's job to induce them to do so. By motivating the leader, the group members motivate themselves in the process.

Employee attitude surveys are now carried out by some of the most forward-looking companies. I have seen some of their samples. I wish I had kept a copy of that questionnaire my two friends and I devised over twenty years ago, to compare. At any rate, the chief executives who are introducing them today are not doing so out of naivety, or self-love or any inferiority complex, but because they estimate they have something of value to learn from them.

To help one's followers to develop and grow in their own right, one is developing new sources of authority, new sources of control, thus laying down the foundations for a potentially better and richer future.

Notes

1 Mary Parker Follett, *Freedom and Coordination*, Management Publications Trust, London, 1949, p. 52.
2 Warren Bennis and Burt Nanus, *Leaders*, Harper & Row, New York, 1985, p. 21.
3 Bennis and Nanus, *Leaders*, p. 21.
4 Mary Parker Follett, *Dynamic Administration: the Collected Papers of Mary Parker Follett*, Elliott M. Fox and L. Urwick, eds, Pitman Publishing, London, 1973, p. 250.
5 Follett, *Dynamic Administration*, p. 232.
6 Follett, *Dynamic Administration*, p. 227.
7 Follett, *Freedom and Coordination*, pp. 56–7.
8 Follett, *Dynamic Administration*, p. 237.

Sourcing Authority and Control: Obeying the Law of the Situation

Management without authority and control is unthinkable except as a recipe for chaos, a sort of *laissez-faire* run riot. But whose authority? Whose control?

The accepted wisdom is that ultimate authority, supreme control, lies with the board of directors. The thinking is that, in every organization, in every social order, there should be a single, ultimate centre of control, some power that is able to pronounce the last word that will be obeyed. Thus, in the business set-up, the board is the locus of all authority and responsibility, the directors delegating them downwards to the selected individuals who will actually carry out the work. Thus, everyone in the company has the authority which has been specifically delegated to them and the responsibility and the right to exercise the control that goes with it.

In this traditional view of the organization, authority and rights, because derived, have to be exercised in accordance with direction. In the final instance, individuals act as directed from above and in turn impose their own direction upon their subordinates. It is essentially based on order taking and order giving. It is a view that did not satisfy me.

The Source of Authority

The kinds of questions that exercised me when I became general manager, with a staff of some four hundred people, were: 'What right have I to manage these people? What right to tell them what to do? What right, in effect, to give them orders?' My colleagues and friends thought my questioning very jejune: 'You have been appointed to the post; that's where your right comes from; stop all this intellectualizing; just get on with the job.' I well knew that I had been appointed to the post and I was indeed getting on with the job. The fact remained, however, that, just as I had always resented taking orders from others, I found it distasteful to give orders to my subordinates.

This was not of course a new experience, the boss/subordinate relation being central to living in society. I had been considered a rebellious child; my children, when small, had been unruly (I had learnt too late that reasoning with very young children does not work, because of their, as yet undeveloped, reasoning capacity); I had felt the myriad gradations of the superior/inferior connection in all other relationships, both private and public. It had been a fact of life which I had coped with more or less successfully. But it became a fact of life which I wanted to understand specifically in relation to the workplace, when I joined at the age of forty the large bureaucratic organization, with clear-cut rules and regulations and established lines of authority.

The Law of the Situation

So, I started delving methodically into the management and related literature, attended seminars and generally brought myself up to date with the then current views on the subject. And, again, it was Follett who provided the most satisfactory answer to my quest: 'One *person* should not give orders to another *person*, but both should agree to take their orders from the situation.'[1]

By developing the concept of 'the law of the situation', Follett at one stroke *depersonalized* orders, removed that objection to the taking and giving of orders which I had long felt and which had surfaced in my new job. The notion was not a new-fangled one. Obeying the law of the situation is a fact of life, something we all do, as a matter of intelligent, thought-out behaviour. Our most appropriate and effective actions are those we take in accordance with what the particular situation demands to be done, according to its own law.

We may or may not like to exercise power. We may or may not want to have responsibility. We may or may not like to give orders. There is one thing, however, which is general to almost all of us: we do not like to *take* orders. We find it demeaning to our integrity, and slighting to our self-esteem. We accept them, when we have to, grudgingly. This unwillingness seems to be instinctive. It is futile to fight against it. Ordering people about in the work-place, or indeed elsewhere, is not entirely successful, for either the giver or the taker.

Follett, studying this fundamental streak of human nature in her usual down-to-earth and analytical way, came to the conclusion that the conundrum of giving and taking orders was a problem we had created for ourselves. She explained that, when a situation is seen in its entirety, it has its own order and its own logic. The authority is inherent in the situation. This internal logic embedded in the situation is 'the law of the situation' which dictates what needs to be done, and both managers and managed are subject to it and take their orders from it. The law of the situation is of general application. When we examine any situation carefully, we find the *significant* facts which then 'speak for themselves' and determine action.

In the work-place, by analysing the relevant situation in detail and as a whole with those involved in it, we can, and will, find its present state of order or disorder and can work out the steps that need to be taken to move it to where we want it to be. Where are we now? Where do we want to get? How do we get there? are the questions which represent the main stages of looking at the present situation, determining where we want it to be and taking the various steps, in their proper order, to take us to it. A critical path analysis charts, in diagrammatic form, the developing pattern of a situation to reach its intended culmination and the dates when various inputs have to be injected and various outputs are expected. It is altered in response to actuality, as contributions and expectations materialize. The analysis diagram acts as an order-giver, everyone involved in that task taking his orders effectively from it, not because A or B arbitrarily says so.

Follett put it quite forthrightly:

Our job is not how to get people to obey orders, but how to devise methods by which we can *discover* the order integral to a particular situation. When that is found, the employee can issue it to the employer, as well as employer to employee . . . If those in supervisory positions should depersonalize orders, then there would be no overbearing authority on the one hand, nor on the other that dangerous *laissez-aller* which comes from the fear of exercising authority. Of course we should exercise authority, but always the authority of the situation.[2]

Well, I had been practising the law of the situation for a long time, in those of my activities which had turned out the most successful. We all do. It was a concept that I could wholeheartedly agree with and that I could adopt consciously, as a tool for effective management. So, it turned out to be. 'Find the law of the situation' became for me an objective which, like 'Find the integrative solution' in resolving conflict constructively, proved invaluable in discovering the true authority which gave the appropriate orders to all, both manager and managed.

As leaders of their team, managers have to understand and visualize the situation, not only for themselves but also, and equally importantly, for those in their group. Managers have their own expertise and the wide vision and understanding, but they are not all-embracing, all-encompassing. The others, too, have their powers of knowledge and experience, of vision and understanding. Their contributions have to be sought, however small, and pooled into the common pot. The final outcome of seeing the situation as it is, as it should be and of the work to be done to get there thus becomes the common enterprise. Each is committed to it in terms of his contribution to the whole. In this way, we *personalize* individual powers but *depersonalize* orders and everyone – from the chief executive to the most subordinate member – can be seen to be taking his orders from the situation itself.

The Subordinate Can Know Better

What I liked best about the concept was the fact that finding the law of the situation did not go all one way, from superior to subordinate; it . could also go the other way, from subordinate to superior. It just depended on who was able to discover the order integral to the situation. Sometimes, subordinates are unwilling to voice their views, because they feel that 'surely, the boss knows this already' but this is not always, or often, the case.

The 'law of the situation' reminded me of an event which had happened very early on, in my first job in the UK, as a translator. My only saleable commodity at that time was a knowledge of languages and the law of my situation then was to work as a translator, whilst training for the accounting profession which would enable me to bring up adequately my two small children. It was yet another irony of life that I had landed a job with a company which acted as agents, selling ships to Brazil. I knew absolutely nothing about ships and

Portuguese was not one of my languages. My job was to translate ships' specifications from Portuguese into English and vice versa. The problem was precariously resolved by the acquisition of a set of multi-lingual technical dictionaries. This was a method not wholly new to me: writing to my English fiancé when I knew no English, I would write my letters in French, then, with the help of a dictionary, translate them into English.

The company had been successful in helping Scottish shipbuilders win an order by open tender for two ships. But this first success had not been followed, subsequent orders going to Holland and Sweden; this was despite all the efforts made on the UK side by all concerned in submitting the most competitive tenders.

At a dinner party in London, the Brazilian delegation, the Scottish directors, the credit providers and various other top people were thrashing out the best way to succeed in the coming tenders. I had been invited, to attend to a minor member of the Brazilian delegation who spoke no English at all. With my French and Spanish and his Portuguese, we could just about communicate. By way of making conversation, I asked him why it was that we were no longer being successful in winning the orders. Well, he explained, 'your people no longer tender strictly according to the specifications we send out. They are always adding improvements. This not only adds to the price but goes against our express requirements. It is also insulting to our professional pride. Such tenders are automatically disqualified. It may be that our specification is not 100 per cent right, but this can be looked at afterwards, if and when you get the order; we could then accept your recommendations or not. The absolute necessity is first to tender strictly according to our specification.' I was surprised; surely, our side knew this. 'We've told them, but they won't listen' was his resigned reply.

I was loth to put this to my boss. I knew that the general consensus on the UK side was that the orders went to those who offered the highest commissions. But perhaps this was not the only overriding condition; perhaps this condition, being invisible, had to be subsidiary to the other, visible, one; one did not exclude the other. After some thinking, I did put what the chap had told me, and my own views, to my boss who, perhaps in desperation, listened. The shipbuilders agreed to draw their quotation more precisely to the specification. I did not leave it at that. Emboldened by my success at having been heard, I went through the quotations very carefully, comparing them with the

Brazilian requirements; they did include for an extra bit here and an extra bit there. I argued with the Scottish designers who said these extra bits were not just cosmetic. 'Never mind that' was my dogged attitude 'Just give them what they want; leave your suggested improvements for inclusion later.' I only sent the quotations when I was fully satisfied that they were in every particular exactly in accordance with the Brazilian specifications and strictly according to the tendering rules. This tender for two ships was won this time by Scotland. The designers were able to incorporate their improvements in subsequent discussions, and the orders for spares that flowed from this order were, according to the shipbuilders, quite phenomenal.

The whole thing had been a simple case of applying 'the law of the situation' by a subordinate who did not know the front from the back of a ship, had not been asked for her opinion, but who had been able to put two and two together more effectively than her superiors, both in rank and in expertise.

The Illusion of Finals

The discrepancy between the received wisdom of that ultimate centre of authority and control and the reality goes back a long way. The notion of derived authority is based on the old idea of sovereignty when the king was the repository of all power and authority which devolved with his release of parcels of land to his followers for services rendered.

In the political field, we have moved on from the autocratic to the democratic form of diffused sovereignty, where the people hold that power and where they elect their representatives to carry out their will. Representatives, however, retain their independence of judgement and action. Once elected, they are responsible for the whole interest of the nation and they owe it to their constituents to exercise freely their best judgement, whether it agrees with theirs or not, unlike delegates who are their principals' agents and have to further their electors' sectional interest.

The difference between a representative and a delegate is crucial. Burke stated the matter very succinctly to his Bristol constituents in 1774:

Parliament is not a congress of ambassadors from different and hostile interests, which interests each must maintain as an agent and advocate, against other agents and advocates; but Parliament is a deliberative assembly of one nation with one interest, that of the whole; where not local purposes, not local prejudices ought to guide, but the general good resulting from the general reason of the whole. You choose a member indeed; but when you have chosen him, he is not a member of Bristol, but he is a member of Parliament.[3]

This may not always happen but the principle at least is enshrined in the written and unwritten constitutions of Western democracies. The elected representatives legislate not for this or that sectional interest but for the best interests of the nation as a whole.

In the business field, we have not yet moved, fairly and squarely, to the democratic form of governance. Directors are by law the trustees of their shareholders' interests, invested with their authority to protect these. The reality is different, for the directors have to, and do, satisfy various other interests. But the fiction remains officially on the books. So does that of delegated authority.

Seventy years ago, Follett was questioning these notions of 'ultimate authority', 'final determination of policy', 'supreme control' and concluding that they were 'a survival of former days'. In any case, they did not fit the ways the then most forward-looking businesspeople actually managed their companies. These individuals did not impose their products or services on the market; they found out what their customers needed or wanted and adjusted their activities to produce them. Externally, they knew they were subject to the control of their customers. Internally, they did not follow indiscriminate 'hire and fire' policies, for they knew that they would always be dependent on those people last hired. They chose their people carefully, trained them, increased their capacities for effective work and ingathered their skills into the total capacity of the business to deliver the right goods or services to the market. In these and many other ways, they were in control, able to satisfy not only the interests of their shareholders but also those of their customers, their workers, their suppliers and the other groups with which they were connected.

In those days there were not many of these far-sighted business-people. The majority of them felt that, as bosses, they had the right to dictate, if not to the market, certainly to their work-force, their suppliers and to any group with less clout than they had. This autocratic way of managing, Follett insisted, could not lead to productive and effective work. Based on the concept that the head was the prime mover of all activity, it was obsolete and did not meet the needs of the then emerging large-scale business enterprise. It is certainly obsolete today.

In every field, in both the physical and the social sciences, the systemic principle is recognized and accepted, the notion of seeing the unit in itself as a whole, always in the making out of the effective interrelatings of its interdependent parts and, at the same time, itself part of the wider system with which it is connected. The company, in itself, is a dynamic unity being made through the interweavings of its various sub-systems; seen in the wider framework within which it operates, it is part of that environment, in reciprocal interaction with it. It is, at the same time, part and whole, depending upon the viewing standpoint, rather like the individual who is a whole in himself and, at the same time, part of the groups to which he belongs. The analogy, incidentally, should not be taken too far. The individual is a whole physical organism, whereas any group, including a business, is made up of separate physical entities, a large difference, too often forgotten by the protagonists of the business-as-organism school.

In the business field, we have moved on, for most productive work, to the concept of the team, a systemic structure; but the organization in place is still, in most companies, the strictly hierarchical form. The outmoded concept of the head retaining responsibility but delegating conditional authority to carry out the work is clung to, not perhaps out of clear conviction, but out of habit – the habit of relying upon assumptions without questioning them to find out whether they remain valid under the new facts.

It is, of course, common knowledge that the work does not get done strictly according to the organization chart. Alongside the pyramidal structure, an informal pattern, meeting the formal one at some points, circumventing it at many others, creates itself to allow for the crucial interlinkings necessary for the performance of the task. Alongside the rule-book, working practices perforce grow which overrule it; when the work-force decides to work 'to rule', not much gets done. Not much would get done either, if everyone in the company decided to work exclusively to their job specification and to the formal lines of authority laid down. But the informal one is simply superimposed on the formal pattern which is not questioned and officially changed to reflect what actually happens; it is kept on the books and the new arrangements continue to grow higgledy-piggledy. Even where the need to restructure is recognized and carried out, the new structure does not prove very much better because in the main it is based on the outgrown and outmoded premise of 'delegated' authority.

Unclear and confused thinking can only lead to confused acting. It is essential to look at the assumptions underlying our ways of working together and to question them. If found wanting, we should replace them with bases more in keeping with our newer knowledge and experience; and also with best practice, which has always a way of running ahead of theory.

This does not mean doing away with the hierarchical system altogether, a mistake that the protagonists of the 'organic' school make. A hierarchical order exists in all living forms, but it is a *relational*, not a *directional*, one. If we see where authority actually lies and who, in fact, are those exercising the power and how they connect with each other, we could organize ourselves for better results. The map is not the territory but it is drawn so that we can find our way in it; so should the structure of the business be devised in such a way as to enable all its workers, managerial and otherwise, to connect effectively.

Real Versus Delegated Authority

It is not difficult to find the true source of authority. 'Just look at the job' was Follett's advice. It is the task, the activity to be carried out, which is the source of the real authority. To be sure, the appointment gives its holder the authority to act, but this authority has no substance outside of the job. Each situation has its own order, its own law. As the task is at the centre of the situation, it follows that it is the task itself, seen in its entirety, which authorizes, dictates, what needs to be done. How well individuals discern this order depends upon their perceptual and deductive skills; how well they implement it depends upon the resources at their disposal and how they use them. Authority belongs to the job and stays with the job; the power to exercise it attaches to the individual posted for the time being to it and the responsibility is his, when he has done it.

Some examples, taken from jobs well down the ladder will illustrate the point. The despatch clerk, as he exercises his function, has an authority over despatching that his manager lacks. He exercises power independently of his manager and, if he exercises it badly, like sending the wrong order, it is too late for the manager to intervene.

Telephonists, *qua* telephonists, often wield more power than the combined forces of many of the people higher up in the hierarchy. At the more dramatic level, when disgruntled workers put pins in the packets of crisps or bits of string in the hamburgers or bug the computer system, they are exercising in no uncertain terms their power. They are, of course, using their power irresponsibly and, when found, will be dismissed and prosecuted, but this will not undo their actions.

Take another example, this time from the top end of the hierarchy. General policy is said to be 'dictated' by the board of directors and functional policies – marketing, production, finance, personnel and so on – have to implement it. In a sense, this is so. But this general policy, if it is to succeed, has itself to be the product of the underlying and interlocking functional capacities. The marketing manager projects the size of the market, but has to take into account the firm's distribution network and whether the production side can effectively make the goods in the required quantities; the production department could make them, but is hampered by obsolescent machinery or lack of the relevant skilled people; and so on. Their linkages and integration are vital. In a very real sense, therefore, the general policy is dictated, in the well-run companies, not only by their boards but also by their functional capacities; and not only by what each can do in isolation but, more importantly, by how they can deliver together, as a whole.

It is the function of the chief executives (and the boards) to develop the grand vision and set the corporate strategy. From their higher vantage point, they can 'read' more accurately the outside environment and thus work out what the business of the company should be, who should be its customers and what will be of value to them. But, in planning the future, they have to start with the actual means, the existing capacities of people, money and materials available to the company. If these are inadequate or inappropriate, they have to arrange for the right ones to be put in place, before 'dictating' the future strategy. Unless they themselves accept the 'dictation' of the actual existing situation in which the company is, their strategy will fail, however right it may be in relation to the outside environment.

This failure to accept, or to determine accurately, the law of the situation and instead to impose their own view very often leads chief executives and their boards of directors to bad, sometimes disastrous, decisions. One company, in the UK, diversified by acquiring a restaurant chain in the USA. Without adequate knowledge of the situation generally and any expertise in the hotel and catering industry in that country, it failed and had to dispose of the chain at a large loss. Another example: a clearing bank, also in the UK, extended its operations by acquiring a banking set-up in the USA but, without the organization to control it from its UK end and without putting into it the management to determine and monitor its activities, it had to dispose of it, again at a huge loss. In both these cases, the directors failed in their grand strategies because they imposed them from the top downwards, without seeking sufficient information of the diverse conditions prevailing in the USA and without ensuring that their company had, in its hands, the people and the expertise essential to implement them. Action has always to go both ways and be integrative. Another company on the other hand succeeds in the USA because it has *in situ* an exceptional chief executive who will only buy those companies where he knows that existing company expertise can turn them round; and he follows knowledge with action by implanting in them the right systems and the right culture. He makes effective and complementary connections between actual capacities.

Quite unwittingly, on appointment from outside as merchandise director of a fashion chain, I walked straight into a situation where the chief executive considered himself all-supreme, the kind that takes it for granted that light will appear as soon as he decrees 'Let there be light.' I knew the company was doing badly and my task was to turn it round, on the merchandise side. I did not know, however, how it was run. I soon discovered that this chief executive ran it by edict, with the other directors as yes-men; he used to refer to them as his poodles. Instead of exercising a restraining influence on his dreams of grandeur, the board, at his behest, had introduced a different business – much more up-market and trendy – in the same outlets. In my visits to the branches, I found the regular customers utterly confused. When they saw the £99.99 skirt alongside its £9.99 counterpart, they thought it was a printing mistake. The selling assistants would explain. The customers would walk out in disgust. The shops could not acquire a new clientele either, for the targeted potential customers would simply not think of buying their clothes in the downmarket outlets of this chain.

There was no way of convincing this chief executive that his strategy was flawed *ab initio*, that consistency was of the essence, that two entirely different businesses could not be run concurrently in the same small outlets and that, in any case, the existing expertise of the chain – buyers, suppliers, sales assistants and so on – was in the run-of-the-mill, mass-merchandising market. He wanted to become known as an up-market retailer; he had engaged me, because of my knowledge of that market, and he thought that the superimposition of just one person would, almost at a stroke, actualize his dream. His persistence at not seeing the logic of the situation led, in the nick of time, to a shareholders' revolt and a boardroom upheaval which saved the company from a take-over or worse.

These examples illustrate the fact that real authority does not flow automatically from the top, from some notional ultimate power. The underlying assumption, so hard to eradicate because not sufficiently questioned, that everything resides at the apex of the pyramid does not tally with reality. Where the notion of delegated authority continues to prevail, the likelihood of loss, small and large, will continue to be ever present.

Personal Responsibility

Real authority then inheres to the task and the power attaches to the individual doing it. Like personal power, it cannot be delegated. Even when the individuals, be they machine operator, or manager, or chief executive, are away and someone else is doing their job in full, there can be no *factual* delegation of authority. A transfer of authority, yes; but no delegation. The transferee has to make the decisions which the job, the situation, demands and, with exactly the same means, will carry the same task differently, in at least some particulars. With the transfer of authority goes the transfer of responsibility; this now attaches to the doer, as to how he does the job. Authority and responsibility go with the task and with the person doing it.

To recognize that every individual carrying out a task for the business, whether inside or outside it and however small it may be, is getting his orders from the task itself, and not from some mythical delegated authority, valorizes individual contributions, changes and dignifies the perception the doer has of his work, and creates in him the desire to do it well, to carry it out responsibly.

Individual authorities and responsibilities are diffused throughout the organization – to those individuals allocated to specific tasks, and not only to the company's own employees but also to those outside whose services the company uses. A business being an interlocking of activities, it follows that individual authorities and responsibilities have to be coordinated and integrated into its collective authority and responsibility to carry out its objectives.

This is the prime function of management. The managerial function of controlling all these activities has never been more crucial and never more demanding. Managers are responsible for the output of their section, department, division. Their function lies in coordinating individual contributions to produce that output and also in connecting the work of their unit with that of the other units of the business. Their function lies therefore in making the members of their team see their specific bit of work as part of the larger scheme of things, of the company's operations. In addition to personal responsibility, they develop in them the sense of collective responsibility and make them see that personal and collective responsibility are bound together and that you cannot have one without the other.

Collective Responsibility

Because of the complexity of today's business, decision making is very much a collective affair. The decision itself may be promulgated by the board of directors or by the relevant authority in the hierarchy, but those making the final decision will not have been its sole authors. A decision is a moment in a process: the moment of decision itself is important, but no more important than all that has gone into its making and all that will flow from its implementation.

Take, for example, a managerial appointment. Most likely, an outside firm of management consultants will have been engaged for the purpose. From the candidates that offer themselves for the post, that firm's interviewer selects those to go forward. Those chosen then have a meeting with a member of the personnel department of the company; at the same time or later, they or some of them meet with their prospective superior; they meet with their potential colleagues and also with some of their subordinates-to-be; meet with the directors and perhaps with the chairman. Finally, one of them will receive the offer of the job, signed, say, by the director of personnel, an offer which he has the power to refuse but decides to accept.

Now, obviously, the director of personnel who signed the offer was not its sole instigator, the sole arbiter of the decision. All the people seen in the company contributed something to the final decision; perhaps it was the subordinates who, preferring that candidate to the others, tilted the decision in his favour. There may be someone who 'finally' may have been responsible for making the decision but it would be difficult to disentangle the exact individual contributions to that decision. It was, in effect, a collective decision, for which those involved are collectively responsible.

In this case, incidentally, whilst it would be difficult to fix specific responsibility for it on anyone in the company, it is clear that the outside interviewer exercised the greatest influence on it, by selecting the applicants to go forward, thus reducing the field of control within which those in the company could make their choice. Thus, someone outside the company, but within it for that specific purpose of selection, exercised a greater authority and power over that decision than anyone in it; and carries therefore the greater responsibility for it.

Further, the final decision – the offer and the acceptance of the job – momentous as it may be to both parties – will only be found to have been right or wrong, or anything in between, through actual performance, through validation in time, itself the product of the means put by the company at the disposal of the appointee and how he uses them.

The appointment of a manager is a relatively simple affair, involving a relatively small number of people. Consider what is required by way of joint effort, of joint responsibility to bring a new product to market, to keep the goodwill and loyalty of one's customers, to introduce new working practices, new machinery. As any activity of the company is analysed, we can see how it interlocks with the others and their mutual interdependence.

Industrial or commercial life is essentially integrated and inter-dependent. All activities, to be successful, are, at the end of the day, joint activities. Joint activity predicates joint responsibility between all in the company. As Follett put it:

we have tended to forget that our responsibility does not end with doing conscientiously and well our particular piece of the whole but that we are also responsible for the whole.[4]

Diffusion and Concentration of Powers

Whilst the trends of increasing specializations and functions are diffusing authorities, others are concentrating them. In one direction, the different conditions in which every business is now operating, where change is occurring so much more quickly than in the past, require that the decisions be made at the point of action. Salespeople, for example, cannot always ask for time to refer to their manager to find out whether they can give the bigger discount or offer the earlier delivery date to clinch an important order. They have to decide as they are negotiating; even a telephone call to their manager would reduce their authority vis-à-vis the potential customer. The thinking and the doing are increasingly combining and moving to the peripheries, to those actually doing the jobs. Decision making, in these cases, is being diffused specifically to the many and becomes their clear-cut responsibility.

In an opposite direction, the use of increasingly complex computer systems and automation is moving authority and control from the many to the one or the few. Machines and systems have replaced human beings but these machines and systems have to be operated at some point by some individuals who are, in effect, personally exercising a power, previously dispersed and divided amongst the many. This places them in positions of authority and control, the extents of which are not always appreciated and the abuse of which cannot be readily or quickly detected.

These opposing trends are found either in their single isolated state or in varying combinations in the same company. Power is being diffused outwards and concentrated inwards: outwards, to those having to make decisions on the spot and inwards, to those controlling operations from their computer bases.

Whether diffused or concentrated, power is now seen to be clearly in the hands of the doers. In trying to control misuse of their powers, which can be very costly, companies are introducing more and more controls. This is not the best answer in the long run.

Organizing for Responsible Work

The best work is that done by the free individual. The true scientist, writer, craftsman, gardener, doctor, is dedicated to the task. They will worry about it until they get it right. They are never satisfied; each new way they find opens possibilities of doing it in still a different and better way. They are said to be a slave to their vocation; therein lies their freedom. They determine their own work, for which they are responsible. Their freedom of action is, of course, highly circumscribed by many factors, including the technology available and their own capacities. However, within the given canons which are fixed for the time being, the doers have degrees of freedom to do the work in whichever way they choose. Responsibility – accepting and working within the existing limitations and, through these, finding the better way and, in due course, reducing the limitations themselves – is the concomitant of freedom.

At work, as it is organized especially for the work-force, the worker is given no such responsibility, no such freedom. Inflexible rules are laid down which have to be followed faithfully. The image of chickens cooped up in their batteries and of workers stuck before their piece of machinery which they have to manoeuvre, in some small way, as the product passes them spells the same message: absence of freedom. People are not robots. They will always want to seek their freedom. The senseless vandalism of putting noxious substances in food products can occur in companies which pride themselves on being enlightened employers, giving good pay and good working conditions but which expect, in return, strict compliance with the work pattern laid down, a design in which the worker has had no say at all. Thrust into the straitjacket of movement and time, the workers' frustration will erupt sometimes, when the limit of their endurance is overtaken by some specific sense of real or imagined injustice, into the act of defiance which causes great damage to the company.

The principle is simple and crystal-clear: if you want work done well, work done responsibly, to increasing levels of good performance, you have to give the workers the responsibility for it. Responsibility is not given when the work parameters are set without their participation. To tell them: 'Do this work exactly this way and in no other way' is not making them responsible for it. Rules, of course, must exist, but they must be rules which the worker has had a hand in making. The workers have the authority and the power to do their job well or badly. If you want them to exercise that power responsibly, then the law of the situation, the logic inherent in your want is to give them the responsibility for the way they do their job, within mutually accepted canons.

People have tremendous potential, if entrusted with responsibility. With responsibility must go knowledge. They are dynamically interactive. Knowledge increases one's sense of responsibility and responsibility heightens one's desire for knowledge. The quality-control circles, mentioned in chapter 5, are firmly anchored on the belief in the possibilities of the individual. They are based not on what he actually can do now, but on his hidden abilities which he can, with training, bring forth. Originally intended for production workshops, the circle idea, because founded on full respect for the individual and appealing to what makes him truly human – his innate aspiration to seek and to find – has now spread to offices, sales departments, warehouses, banks, insurance companies; Q-C circles are formed between parent companies and their affiliates and sub-contractors and, in exceptional cases, between rival companies to settle some common problem in their industry.

A method of working together, based on openness, spreading and sharing of knowledge, cooperation and personal responsibility, can be worked out and it will be most effective. When people become knowledgeable and are given freedom to think and act in their own right, they become initiators of their own work. They become involved in wanting to learn more about it, and how they can do it better. They develop greater personal and collective responsibility. I like very much what a very successful company, manufacturing semi-conductor devices in the USA, puts into its work ethic statement: 'The concept of assumed responsibility is accepted. If a task needs to be done, assume you have the responsibility to get it done.' This energizes and inspires, quite the opposite of the deadening effect of being told exactly what to do, and nothing more.

To rely on the personal responsibility of people to do their work well is to trust them. This is to take the risk that it will be abused. Human nature being what it is, some individuals will misuse it for their own ends. This happens in any case in the most tightly controlled companies. In terms of comparative costs, to work on the basis of mutual trust is cheaper than to organize it with a panoply of controls. And who controls the last controllers?

Trust is cheaper than mistrust and brings out the best in people. Trusting people is fun. I also think it necessary to personal growth. The mistrusting person is a diminished, and diminishing, individual. Always protecting his back, he can seldom go forward. As with the individual, so with the company. A company which sets up strict systems of control, according to which actions have to be carried out and assessed, soon gets so entangled in them that it becomes immobilized, and effectively their prisoner. That fine company which tells its people to assume responsibility for any task that they consider needs to be done is undeniably trusting them that they will do it right. It is also giving them the opportunity to act and, through doing, to grow. Of course, the trusting person will be let down sometimes; this is a fact of life that one simply takes in one's stride. The working theory I use is that the trusting person, or the trusting company, is let down less often than the mistrusting person or company which takes, in every case, the most careful precautions to protect itself.

Imposed control is less effective than self-control, or, to be more exact, the control that is exercised on us by our peers. The individual, made responsible for his work which he has helped to shape, will want to do it right and well. But he may, he will, slacken. We are all fallible and likely to fall by the wayside now and again. But he will slacken less if he is a member of a team, where his activity is clearly visible to the others, whose own work depends on his. He will not risk doing it badly, for fear of their disapproval. What we really care about is what our peers think of us. More than hierarchical control, pay or promotion, our colleagues or workmates influence our behaviour. They support us of course but they also control us, in direct and in other subtle intangible ways. In the team, there is mutual support and also mutual control, the most natural and, therefore, most effective means of achieving worthwhile work.

The Individual Manager's Authority

It is usually held that changing the culture of a company from the directorial to the cooperative one has to be initiated by top management; otherwise, it can have no chance of success. This is not a tenable proposition, if you accept the premise that not all authority and all control reside in the apex of the pyramid and flow from it. Top managements can be indoctrinated and perhaps be convinced that the cooperative method is more effective and can even set up the relevant systems, but nothing much will change if either their habit-patterns or those of the individuals at the relevant power-points have not changed. Consider, for example, the non-discriminatory policies followed by most companies. Yet, we find very few women in positions traditionally held by males. Why? Because, in the main, those in actual authority, whether in the personnel department, or the department where the woman would be employed, or the directors themselves find numerous, apparently valid, reasons to prefer the old type of incumbent. They cannot act contrary to life-long habits. They cannot change them by order.

To change the culture of a company, management consultants have found, to their profit and at corresponding large cost to their client companies, that the indoctrination and the habit-changes have to be infiltrated throughout the organization and have to permeate it. All layers in the company have to have their brainstorming sessions, their week-end get-togethers, their training programmes, their audit schedules and so on; confirmation, if confirmation were needed, that authorities and powers cannot be delegated from above, but lie with tasks and in the individuals doing them.

Irrespective of what is going on in top management, individual managers can turn the members of their group into the achieving team. They can introduce the cooperating method and make it prosper. The authority is theirs, by virtue of their task. It is true that they are constrained by the organization, by its culture and the systems in place which have to be followed. Within these limitations, however, the individual managers have the right and the power to initiate. Within their province, they can redefine vague job descriptions, clarifying individual responsibilities; they can involve their people in the preparation of their budgets; discuss with them actual performance against budget; make the people their own quality controllers; give them time off to go and see a trade exhibition, a customer's factory, or look at the competition. They can get the group's views on whether or not to instal new machinery; listen to what they have to say; get them to set up their own individual standards; the managers can make them fit their individual part in the whole, not only in the company but also in the whole comprising the company in its environment. In dozens of ways, and all the more effective because specific to the task, managers can use the actual, and help develop the potential, capacities of those in their group. As they do this, the group will undoubtedly achieve more. As the leader succeeds and achieves more, it is most likely that his peers will want to copy his methods; and the practical value of these methods can thus spread, organically, throughout the company. Through actual performance, the managers, however subordinate they may be in the ladder they are, can become agents for productive change in the company. Change can come from below as well as from above.

When Follett was writing, seventy years ago, about joint power and joint responsibility, managers and managed formed, in the majority of cases, two watertight, separate classes. Managers were employed to think, workers hired as 'hands'. If the workers showed any initiative, they were bluntly told: 'You're paid to work, not to think.' The notion that they had as much power and as much responsibility as their managers for the well-being of the company as a whole was unacceptable to both parties.

The notion is less unacceptable now but it has still a long way to go. It is bound to come, for the logic of the situation demands it. The personal responsibility of everyone in the business and their collective responsibility is a must for the success of the enterprise, as well as for each one in it. It is not a welfarist notion but a plain necessity, a central part of the strategy that will distinguish, between companies, the leaders from the laggards.

The thoughtful managers can lead today and show the way ahead by establishing in their section or department that mode of association in which joint activity can take place and collective responsibility take root and grow, making for work of a high, and highly satisfying, order.

Notes

1 Mary Parker Follett, *Dynamic Administration: the Collected Papers of Mary Parker Follett*, Elliott M. Fox and L. Urwick, eds, Pitman Publishing, 1973, p. 30.
2 Follett, *Dynamic Administration*, p. 30.
3 Edmund Burke, Speech to the electors of Bristol, 3 November 1774.
4 Follett, *Dynamic Administration*, p. 51.

8

The New Managers:
The Societal Leaders

We are living in truly exciting times, fluid and volatile and so fast-changing that 'we see the present when it is already disappearing'. Up to early 1989, conditions in Europe, although seen as uncertain, were in general terms clear-cut. Europe was divided into two main sectors, the Western European Community and the Soviet Union with its Eastern European bloc. For those in the European Community, the advent of the single European market in 1992 was to be the apogee of their evolution and all efforts were directed to finding a *modus operandi* in the new environment being developed.

The fall of the Communist governments in the countries of Eastern Europe, one after the other over a few months in late 1989, dramatically changed the political face of Europe, and, therefore, of the world. It is no exaggeration to say that it was due in the main to one man, Mikhail Gorbachev, who, impelled by the failure of the Soviet economy, decided to change its foreign policy. The Soviet Union could no longer sustain the financial demands of a military superpower; recognizing this fact, Gorbachev decided that the old familiar East–West adversarial confrontation was to be no more. It was this decision that gave the signal to East Germany, Hungary and Czechoslovakia that the Soviet Union no longer intended to use its troops to enforce its will on them. The peoples, sensing this, rose and toppled their governments. Thus, the Soviet bloc disintegrated.

In writing, in chapter 4, about the integrative solution as the best means of resolving conflict. I said that, at the extreme, if I find the solution that fully meets your demand, what will there be left for us to fight about? In this case, Gorbachev saw what the law of the situation for the Soviet Union was. This gave him the courage to proclaim it both in words and in deeds, at least in sufficient deeds to bring the Cold War to an end. Gorbachev found the solutions that went more than half way to meet the West's demands and, as a result, the Cold War was over. An individual by his own unilateral actions can make a difference.

The New European Environment

The Cold War is over but the changes resulting from Gorbachev's initiatives are monumental. Their full repercussions are difficult to foresee. They will be different in each country of the former Eastern European bloc, each with its different history and with the different arrangements it succeeds in developing with Western Europe and the rest of the world. In all of these countries, however, the aim is clear: to move to a democratic form of government and to convert from a command to a market economy.

The difficulties are very great. The politicians can establish the right macro-economic framework and capital can be found but these prerequisites of success are not sufficient in themselves. After some forty-five years of economic activity directed by the Communist party and by the state, there are no infrastructures in place in these ex-satellite countries to facilitate the move from one system to another and the peoples themselves are not conversant with the workings and the constraints of a free-market economy. Appropriate organizations have to be created and appropriate modes of behaviour acquired. It is in these areas that Western European businesspeople and managers can and will be of great value: in helping the local entrepreneurs to set up the organizations and advising them on how best to run them.

In the Soviet Union, the problems are more complex. Communism there, as an indigenous institution of some seventy years' standing, has a much greater hold on everyone, and cannot be as summarily dismissed as it has been in the other Eastern European countries. The political–economic conundrum in the Soviet Union is further compounded by demands for independence by important ethnic populations. Nevertheless, the pressure of popular demand and of events is creating its own logic which is liberalizing the political system and which must liberate the running of the economy from its state shackles. Here again, and in this optimistic scenario, the contribution of Western businesspeople in creating and running the private sector will be a crucial condition of success.

Despite the difficulties and the problems, foreseen and unforeseen, the new aspirations of the peoples in the Eastern European countries and in the Soviet Union are for 'a common European home'; that closed world is to be closed no more. Ideally, free trade within the single European market will be conducted with these countries, each wanting to join in the bounties which appear to flow from a free-market economy.

Suddenly, there appears the likelihood of a new European order. Suddenly, the advent of the single European market in 1992 is no longer the high point of Europe's future. There is a great deal more before and beyond 1992, both for the whole of Europe and for the world. Suddenly, the single European market in 1992, is changing in purpose to become but a stepping-stone to yet greater things. A whole new range of possibilities opens up for a 'greater Europe'.

The New Challenges for Business

In his report to the NATO members in early December 1989, President George Bush was quite clear that Gorbachev 'absolutely mandates new thinking'. If Gorbachev mandated new thinking in the military arena, the political changes themselves absolutely mandate new thinking in the business field. The prospect of the single European market of 1992 was concentrating the minds of the business leaders on how best to adjust to the changing nature of their activities; they were preparing themselves for their wider freedoms for trade and investment and also for the more intensive resulting competition. They were moving in relatively uncharted seas but the European Commission was there in Brussels, acting as the central authority, harmonizing differences and providing the new rules of the game.

Political events in Eastern Europe have suddenly and immeasurably widened the opportunities and the challenges for business managers and leaders in the EC – and also their responsibilities. For the time being, at any rate, most of the populations in Eastern Europe, having experienced the bankruptcy of government-led economic activity, are starry-eyed about the benefits of our political and economic system. They have an idealized picture of life in a liberal democracy, where, to them, all appears to be just and fair. And, for them, the profit motive of the free-market economy has somehow been elevated into the miraculous instrument which will almost automatically and immediately ensure the appearance in their shops of those necessities they have been denied for so long. Their current uncritical acceptance of the political and economic system in Western Europe should not induce in its capitalists a triumphalist or a complacent attitude. Our economic system has indeed won because it delivers the goods much more effectively than does the Communist system of centralized direction and control but not everything in the free-market economy is perfect. Winning should not blind us to its shortcomings.

In Eastern Europe, the requirement is to improve the standard of living of the people in each country on a continuing basis. To this end, apart from the money which is not the biggest problem, they also need the technological, marketing and managerial know-how of Western European businesspeople. Without this specific contribution, the political upheavals there could have no liberal tomorrows. A market economy demands a democratic form of government and conversely democracy cannot take root and prosper unless it is backed by a free enterprise economy which meets reasonably successfully the material demands of its people. The economic and political system is an indissoluble whole. Thus, it will devolve upon the businessmen and managers to make a major contribution to the establishment of a new democratic European order which the politicians alone could never achieve.

Already, the single European market of 1992 was making business leaders re-examine their objectives and strategies. Now, because of the unexpected developments in the rest of Europe and the exciting prospects of a 'greater Europe' and of a 'common European home', it is all the more imperative for them to re-assess in depth their aims and determine the full purpose of their business activities.

If they do not do this, if they go into the new emerging order with their business ethic of maximizing profits and only concentrating on this, they will fail. They will be letting down not only themselves and their shareholders but also those people dependent upon them for a better world and, by extension, the rest of us. The example of Latin America is out there for all to see. Billions of dollars were poured in many Latin American countries, for large-scale projects intended to improve the lot of the common people. But their living conditions remain as miserable as ever and, in some cases, have become worse. The bankers and the entrepreneurs went for maximization of their profits, leaving it to the free market 'trickle-down' effect to reach the populace. There has, in fact, been very little trickling down of benefits. On the other hand, there has been a large flow of austerity measures from the governments, having to meet interest and debt repayments. And these, as usual, bear most harshly on the people.

The Prince of Wales, as President of Business in the Community, in February 1990, at a business forum looking at the opportunities arising in Eastern Europe put it quite bluntly:

Business is at a crossroads – does it enter the new markets like the cowboys of the new frontier? Or does it take a rather more sophisticated approach which leads to continued rather than short-term profit – and in doing so makes provision for future generations and future stake-holders?

The business leaders must ensure it is the latter.

The Need for a Philosophy

Businesspeople have not remained unaware of the need to have wider aims than those strictly laid down in their business ethic. Indeed, the Business in the Community organization was set up, in 1981, to enable its members to fulfil these wider aims. For a number of years now, the major companies in the UK have taken to stating their 'philosophy' or as some put it 'their mission' in their annual reports to shareholders. A typical example reads:

- To provide a high standard of product and service to our customers at fair prices.
- To provide our employees with the security of working for a successful company with job satisfaction, good remuneration and good working conditions, acknowledging their right to be informed and consulted on all matters which affect their work.
- To earn sufficient money after tax to provide an adequate return on the savings that our shareholders have entrusted to our care, after reinvesting enough capital in the business to maintain the value of their assets and to ensure the healthy long-term growth of the company.
- To conduct our business with due care for the environment and for the interests of the consumer and the general public.

This is excellent as far as it goes: good public relations. But it will not help the manager in decision making within the ambit of each commandment unless he knows the assumptions underlying it and the reasons built on those assumptions. He must be able to answer the questions: Why? How? When? Collectively or singly? And so on.

Let us take the first precept quoted above: 'To provide . . . at fair prices.' Now, what is a 'fair' price? Is this a subjective concept? Is it 'fair' to offer considerable discounts to the bulk purchaser and not to the small man already at a competitive disadvantage? Is it possible, in practice, to do otherwise? Is it 'fair' to charge the same price to the trader in an impoverished inner-city area as to one in the prosperous South East? Is it, or is it not, 'fair' to the different customers to have a differential area trading price? Does a 'fair' export price result from taking advantage of differential exchange rates? Does the price stay 'fair' when it is maintained after the suppliers' prices have plummeted? And so on.

In this particular 'philosophy' statement, relations with one's suppliers are not covered but, in terms of fairness to one's suppliers, is it 'fair' for the large company to take advantage of its small suppliers by not paying them on time, on the due dates? This is the perennial complaint of the small firms dealing with the large companies, many of which proudly proclaim their mission of fairness in their annual reports.

How 'fair' is a company in its dealings with its customers? Do not many companies have in fact different degrees of fairness between customers? The strong customer, in knowledge or money or similar muscle, is indeed treated with every consideration and very fairly, but the weak customer who cannot answer back is short-changed with the inferior or inappropriate good or service and persuaded that he is buying the best. The alleged case of unethical marketing by Nestlé, selling their powdered milk – no longer wanted in the West – to third world countries has been well publicized. How many businesspeople, with unsold obsolete or obsolescent stocks will now try to sell them to Eastern European customers as the ultimate in technology that the West has to offer?

In fact, one could go on dissecting every maxim of this type of company's 'philosophy'. It goes without saying that the managers will know their business, know their market, know their competition. But such knowledge alone will not help them to find the right answers unless they know the assumptions on which the thinking is based and the reasoning which has led to the enunciation of the rules.

Staff relations and the rules which govern them require exactly the same understanding of the hidden assumptions and the reasoning on which the rules are based. Rules by themselves are not always all that helpful. Under the rules a manager may, for example, delegate a task to one of his subordinates. Why? To lighten his own work load? To test the subordinate's competence? To teach him to take responsibility? Probably, a bit of all this and more. I was with the managing director on one occasion when a member of his staff came into the office with a file and announced: 'I have drafted two replies for your consideration, one which I would like to send and another which perhaps we ought to send.' The MD, a shrewd and kindly fellow, looked at neither and said: 'Which am I to sign?' The young man went away to produce another draft: one which he could present to his boss without question or qualification and one which the MD would sign with perhaps a surreptitious peep at its contents. That MD was a psychologist who did not rely on hierarchical protocol but used his own common sense and philosophy. He knew that it was not only improper but also counter-productive and confidence-destroying to delegate authority with one hand and withdraw it with the other.

The primordial need for businesspeople and managers is to clarify and spell out the criteria and assumptions underlying their statements of intent and their actions – to declare the values underpinning their thinking, their behaviour, their ways of doing business. We can only act on the basis of what we think about human nature and the view we take of human beings. We use these beliefs all the time, whether we recognize the fact or not. They may be covert, but they are there, and determining our behaviour all the same. Some of our ideas and beliefs may contradict one another; these contradictions, unbeknown to us, will be reflected in our behaviour which, as a result, will itself be lacking in coherence and, accordingly, be that less effective.

Businesspeople, managers, will function better, be more effective and successful, if they uncover their hidden agendas, put their beliefs and values in context with each other and fashion them for themselves into some kind of wholesome order, always in accordance with actual and potential reality. It is then that they can integrate their analytical skills and logic that much better with their intuitive and 'gut' feelings which leads to the coherent vision and the consistent action. Thus, leaders can develop a philosophy which provides them with a rich and balanced foundation from which they can view the influence of the past on the present and project the present into the future. Thus, they evolve the critical attitude that seeks answers to questions like:

- What are we in business for?
- Who is or what is the company?
- What are the principles actuating our behaviour now? What should they be? What could they be?
- To whom are we, as directors and/or managers, truly responsible?
- What is the role of our company in society? What could it be?

Every question brings other questions, opens vistas and widens the scope of endeavours and activities. And this philosophy will not be one which the manager will have evolved on his own but one which he will share and develop with the others, so that it becomes the common and joint philosophy, always growing and changing out of its own, central, inner strength.

The Many-faceted Nature of Human Beings

There are very few professions or callings for which a knowledge of people is not of considerable and even prime importance. Management is certainly not one of the exceptions. But basic to this practical consideration is the deeper question: what view do managers take, should they take, of human beings? The way in which they answer this question, which managers always do even if only implicitly, determines the way they look at the world and the place of human beings in it. This leads them to their professional judgements: what sort of business organizations they create and the way in which they operate within them.

The philosophers through the ages have addressed themselves to this basic question. Not to go too far back into history, Hobbes, in the seventeenth century, took the view, in the frequently quoted passage, that 'man is a wolf to man' and that, without a state that is supreme in regulating the relations between individuals, there would be 'no arts; no letters; no society; and, which is worst of all, continual fear of violent death; and the life of man solitary, poor, nasty, brutish and short'. (The wags have always retorted that it could be worse: nasty, brutish and long.) His view of man led him to counsel the dictatorial state, all for the good of the individual. The dictatorial state has invariably failed the individual.

The behaviourists, coming nearer in time to us, give us different interpretations. At the beginning of this century we had Pavlov and his salivating dogs. He rang a bell and, immediately on ringing the bell, he gave the dogs some food. In due course, he trained the dogs so well that they would salivate at the sound of the bell, whether or not there was food. From this, he developed the stimulus–response theory which, extrapolated to human behaviour, informs the carrot and whip motivation theory: if we behave nicely, that is in accordance with what our superiors want us to do, we get a reward, the carrot; if not, we get the telling off and, in due course, the boot, that is, the whip.

Today, very much still with us, we have Skinner, the great rat protagonist. He has spent his life working on rats and extrapolates human behaviour from what he has found his rats do, when he lets them loose in their mazes, or in the numberless other experiments to which he subjects them. One gets the impression that the term 'rat race' now so commonly applied to various human activities, such as acquiring and spending, or struggling for supremacy in the business world, and so on, has emanated from some of Skinner's experiments. Somehow, rats have infected behaviour especially in the business field, where it is now, for some, almost a matter of professional pride to behave as rats are assumed to do.

Homo economicus was an invention of the economists as a sort of yardstick for the measurement of economic behaviour. It was only a hypothesis, in that they just saw him behaving 'as if' he was 'economic' in the decisions they decided to study, but the 'as if' got quickly forgotten about and man became wholly enshrined into 'economic man'. I still remember the lecturer's pronouncement, at a seminar at the London School of Economics, when I hesitatingly questioned the axiom of 'economic man'. 'Madam', he said in his most withering tones, 'we are here to study Economics, not to speculate upon the nature of man.'

The descriptive economists from Adam Smith onwards certainly did not disregard the complex nature of man, but many of the modern analytical economists get close to doing exactly that. Their addiction to pure mathematical analysis has vitiated so many economic predictions that it is small wonder that, of all the disciplines, economics is the most discredited. The reputation of economists in public esteem generally seems to be at about the same level as that suffered by meteorologists before satellite photography came to their aid. The hubris of the economists is that they persist in abstracting man into that economic animal which he simply is not and in wanting to explain all human behaviour, including the actions of the missionary and the philanthropist, exclusively in strict cost–benefit analysis. No wonder that a committed number of people, including amongst them some economists, in rebelling against the reductionism of this dismal science, are developing the new economics, based on a more comprehensive view of economic activity.

The nature of man is far too complex to abstract into one aspect or to circumscribe into a few specific elements. Many views have been propounded from time to time but they change in important ways as knowledge in the different disciplines advances. Knowledge is never hermetic; new understandings in one branch of knowledge seep through to affect the views of the subjects in another. Advances in physics, for example, have impacted on psychology and thence on the views of the nature of man. This happened when the physicists abandoned their views on the machine-like nature of the universe in favour of the hologram-like concept which is based on the complex interconnections of systems and of the systemic part itself having enough information of the whole to be able to recreate it, albeit not in fullest detail.

In psychology, this has had the effect of replacing the view of the individual as a single isolated self attempting self-mastery, with that of the individual achieving harmony through integrating his various tendencies, and also interacting effectively with his psychological environment. There is no question now of suppressing any one characteristic but of putting them all in their proper relational order, which is just as difficult as the earlier endeavour, but more wholesome.

The essential point about this is that one should abandon the idea that a personality is made up of any one main instinct or trait, conveniently ignoring all the others, in favour of the view which accepts the individual in his full diversity. Selfishness and greed, for example, are part of human nature, but only a part. There is no sense or value in either elevating them into the sole springs of human behaviour or in suppressing them and denying their existence. This is to fall into the trap of the either/or attitude which polarizes, opposes and is always reductionist. It is more realistic to accept both selfishness and greed as components of human nature and channel their force into one's long-term advantage.

Managers will have their own feelings and attitudes on all this; some will not go along with the new thinking, but the course advocated here is that they should: they should take a 'whole' view of the individual and see them as a complex interactive being, not all good and not all bad, not all angel or all beast; a mixture of instincts, prejudices, emotions, desires, aspirations; heart, mind and will combining differently in each individual to make them the unique being they are.

There are two practical advantages that stem immediately from this outlook. The first is personal, in that the approach is useful in terms of self-development in working towards the better-integrated personality, and it is also helpful in enabling one to establish a code of personal behaviour in a social and psychological setting. The second is related to the first in that it provides a basis for understanding and appreciating others and working out effective ways in which one deals with those others. Both work to make for the more effective manager.

In the managerial context, as indeed in any context which involves human relations, it is most important to achieve respect and understanding on a reciprocal basis for those with whom one is associated. One cannot hope to influence, persuade, or convince those one despises or towards whom one is indifferent; and the converse is equally true. For many, moralist and pragmatist, to respect others as oneself is the basis of all human relationships. Where there is mutual respect, there will be no sharp dealing, no tendency to push the weak to the wall. Accepting the others in their complexity, respecting them for what they are and what they can become, treating them *with respect* brings out the most constructive traits in them. It makes working together an enjoyable experience and a fruitful endeavour, much more so than when we treat each other as mere economic units, or rats or salivating dogs. Human nature being what it is, every one falls by the wayside at some time and commits the underhanded or cowardly action of which they cannot be proud. But the basic principle of respect for the other remains the beckoning light, a principle which we are now learning has to extend beyond all living things to include the environment; without such respect, we turn even apparently inanimate matter against us.

Seeing the actual in its reality does not mean accepting the *status quo*; it means understanding it and working with it so as to be able to change it in the desired direction. What is unique about man is his culture which he can pass on. We *can* evolve better ways of dealing with each other. Follett, in her usual incisive way, could see that 'the goal of evolution most obviously must evolve itself'.[1] We do evolve. Richard Dawkins, the ethologist/biologist, in *The Selfish Gene* mentioned in chapter 1, developed the concept of the 'meme' (which he says is pronounced to rhyme with cream) to explain man's cultural transmission which goes on alongside his genetic transmission. Examples of memes are tunes, fashions, catch-phrases, ideas and so on. Anyone can pass on an idea he has; if it catches on, it spreads from brain to brain: 'Memes should be regarded as living structures, not just metaphorically, but also technically.' Ideas get implanted and transmit themselves as surely and as permanently as do genes. The soup of human culture, as Dawkins refers to cultural transmission, 'is achieving evolutionary change at a rate that leaves the old gene panting far behind'.[2]

Interestingly enough, in his second edition of the book, published in 1989, Dawkins has added much new material and has updated his 1976 position. He now has an additional chapter on 'Nice guys finish first', based on what is called the tit-for-tat strategy. So, however red in tooth and claw nature may be, we can learn to work with it. We can be '*nice*' and also '*come first*'. Richard Dawkins, for one, has certainly evolved in his views. And Robert Axelrod in his book *The Evolution of Co-operation* goes further and finds even cooperation in biological systems:

Cooperation in biological systems can occur even when the participants are not related, and even when they are unable to appreciate the consequences of their own behaviour. What makes this possible are the evolutionary mechanisms of genetics and the survival of the fittest . . . Darwin's emphasis on individual advantage can, in fact, account for the presence of cooperation between individuals of the same or even different species.[3]

The Many-faceted Nature of the Business Enterprise

In the new millennium that augurs the coming of age of management, the time has come to dispense with the outmoded, but still persisting, theory of the firm which abstracts it exclusively into an economic entity. It is indeed time to move to the view which reflects more fully the reality and recognizes the business enterprise as a complex human organization, encompassing social, political, and moral, as well as economic, activities. Taken only as an economic unit, a business will perform as inadequately as the 'economic man' performs. Andrew Ure, the prototype management consultant, was already writing in the early 1800s in his book, *The Philosophy of Manufacturers*, that economic theory does not motivate anyone and that employers had to attend to the moral machinery of their factories as carefully as they attended to their engineering facilities.

Although doing good work in the community has now become a mandatory activity for any self-respecting company and 'Our work in the community' takes a prominent place in its annual report, a company seldom sees itself, or is regarded by its members, as a community. Yet, it is indeed, itself, a community. Success in manufacturing or service industries is based essentially on the ability to survey the market closely and provide the product or service that meets the market's needs competitively as to price, performance and service. To achieve this requires close and intimate cooperation amongst all the workers in the enterprise. If the business is in manufacturing, for example, the cooperation is needed not only in the production-related areas of research, development, design and manufacturing, but also in the associated areas of marketing, distribution, accounting and after-sales service. To do this effectively requires harmonizing operations and attitudes through all corporate activities. This entails management or social engineering to create the work-groups where cooperation (which does not exclude tension and conflict) can develop.

Each work-group is a nuclear community in its own right, which the manager together with its members are creating anew out of the multifarious happenings affecting them each working day; as a work-group, it connects with the other groups in the company and, together, they form its internal and immediate community. But the organization is not only this limited community; it consists also of its suppliers, its customers, all the companies with which it has ties, its shareholders, bankers and to a certain extent too, its competitors.

The business is the hub of networks of different categories of people, each category contributing something to their specific common end and receiving something in return. The main exchanges between these various categories are made on the basis of money but they are not all exclusively or mainly economic. The relations between members of the work-group or those between different departments in the company are essentially social in character, with all that this involves in terms of cultural, emotional, political, and moral content; people bring their prejudices, emotions and aspirations as well as their skills to the performance of their work, whatever it may be.

A business is effectively a social organization in which individuals are collaborating to pursue economic activities of benefit to the larger community as well as to the groups within. It is that fact of reciprocation which is important, which validates one's work and gives it meaning. Human beings need bread but they also need to have meaning in their lives. The founders of the great enterprises always understood this and organized their businesses in such a way that the people in them 'had something to live for as well as something to live by'. This was the aim of John Spedan Lewis (1885–1963), when he formed the John Lewis Partnership, that uniquely successful example of industrial democracy. As he wrote in his book *Fairer Shares*: 'The supreme purpose of the John Lewis Partnership is simply the happiness of its members. True happiness requires a sense of honest service to the general community, a sense of being of some use to the world.'[4] Konosuke Matshushita (1895–1989), the exemplar of Japan's post-war industrial success, was saying the same thing in his credo that 'People need a way of linking their productive lives to society' and was doing the same thing, albeit in a different form of organization, when he enriched the lives of those who worked in it in material well-being as well as in meaning.

The different facets of the total activity of the business are not separable or sequential. A company does not attend to its economic purpose, then decide on the form of organization it needs. The two go hand in hand; productivity and profitability depend upon the organization set up to carry out the activity; such organization, relating human beings to one another, can only be social. A company does not first fulfil its economic responsibility to its employees by giving them good pay and working conditions and then attend to its social or moral responsibility by adding meaning to the work. The meaning is already extant in the form of organization the company, through its managers, has designed for itself. A strictly hierarchical form of organization based on the 'I command, you do as I say' principle diminishes all the individuals in it, thereby reducing their development; and, by the same token, reduces their present and potential contribution to the company, thus affecting its performance. The economic activity of the company is itself embedded in morality. Even the strictest interpretation of the business ethic to maximize profits only recognizes that this has to be achieved without fraud and within the confines of the law, itself based on the prevailing ideas of justice and fairness of the times, and themselves subject to evolution.

Yet, the idea of separatedness goes deep; even Peter Drucker, who has done so much to promote business to its rightful place in society, writing in 1968 in *The Practice of Management* strongly felt that:

The company is not and must never claim to be home, family, religion, or fate for the individual. It must never interfere in his private life or his citizenship. He is tied to the company through a voluntary and cancellable contract, not through some mystical and indissoluble bond.[5]

Certainly, no worker wants to be grappled to his employing company with 'hoops of steel' and certainly he is not tied to it 'through some mystical or indissoluble bond' but, irrespective of any claims that either employer or employee may want to make, the factory floor, the office, the space one occupies for so many hours a day is physically one's day-time abode. Real time, real life is had in any place where people spend some thirty to forty hours a week pursuing any kind of activity earning a living. We don't just work to make a living; we also spend a considerable amount of time living at work. Work is part of life, not something separate from it. Our place of business is where we work and where we also live. I was not so wide of the mark when I told the people in the store that it was our day-time home, to be fashioned by us for most effective working and living.

In reality, work-life and private-life cannot be kept separate; they spill into each other; an unhappy private life impinges on one's work and difficult relations at work redound on one's behaviour at home. An urgent deadline at work has to be met by encroachment upon one's private time and an emergency at home requires interference in company time. The aim is not that the twain never meet but that they mesh with, and enrich, each other. And this is best achieved, when the individual is outward-looking and is connecting not only work-life and private-life but also connecting these to his activities in the other groups to which he belongs.

Citizenship is similarly indivisible. There cannot be two standards: one which individuals will assume in their business dealings, based as the cynics would have it on the injunction of 'Make money – honestly, if you can' and another, on fairness or generosity, for one's private relations. Habits acquired in the work-place cannot be discarded and left there, to be worn again on returning to it. If one cuts corners in one's business dealings, one perforce and very soon also does the same in one's private dealings. If one lacks respect for the others at work, that same attitude will insidiously work itself in one's behaviour at home. Integrity is integral to the individual. Without integrity in the work-place, we cannot have integrity in our lives.

Drucker was, of course, anxious to preserve this very integrity, so that individuals did not become mere company fodder. William H. White, in *The Organization Man*, a few years earlier in 1956, had vividly alerted us to the mediocrity of the individual who identifies himself too closely with his group, his team, his company. But identification with one group, say one's work-place, should not inhibit one from identifying with other groups; on the contrary, the more groups an individual joins and participates in, the richer he is as an individual and the greater his contribution to any one of them.

Then, there is also the fear that organizations may take over and impose their interests over those of the wider society. Kenneth Boulding and J. K. Galbraith are writers who warn us of these existing risks and of the importance of providing countervailing powers by way of governmental action. It is true that power corrupts; the more power a company has, the more blinkered it can become. But the correctives should be provided by competition in the market place and by the people in the company itself who, by their daily vigilance and in their daily work, should control the activities of the company to ensure its proper interest which can never run, when fully understood, against the social interest. The control should be in-house, exercised by the followers on their leaders, and mutually between the followers themselves.

The Profit Motive

Business and the profit motive have, on the whole, had a bad press through the ages. The tradition has been that the artist, the scientist, the craftsperson, the professional individual are motivated by the love of their work, their search for excellence and their devotion to standards. 'Professional honour', 'professional integrity' actuate their behaviour. The professions are for service. Businesspeople, on the other hand, have been thought to have few standards, if any, their one aim being to make money. Time was, in the last century, when idealists like William Morris were dreaming of a new society. Profit, like money generally, was seen as the root of all evil. The thought carried on into our own day: if only the state, instead of money-grubbers, were running industry, there would be no need for profits. The expression 'profit-motive' became, like 'elitism', a dirty word.

However, the disillusionment with the performance of nationalized industries ushered in a renewed interest in the virtues of private enterprise, and not only in the UK. Profits are now seen for what they are: a necessity for the creation and the continuance in business of all the industries and services on whose output society depends. That a business has to make a profit in order to survive is now generally accepted as necessary. Without an excess of current revenue over current cost, there is no money left to secure the future. Profit is a requirement, a necessity of the business. All organizations, and not only those in business in the private sector, are constrained by economic considerations. Universities, hospitals, charities, in their social work of education, or healing, or relieving poverty and other handicaps, are *ipso facto* concerned also with economic ends: to survive and thus carry on that work, they have to ensure revenues greater than costs over time. These monies can of course be given to them, but the wealth has still to be created by individuals. Today, with the debacle of the government-led economies in the USSR and its bloc, the profit motive is recognized as fulfilling an essential function in the creation of wealth and economic well-being.

The profit motive may have, as they say, come out of the closet but it still lacks full respectability. The tradition still sticks that the service motive of the professions and the profit motive of business are divergent, that the first is superior to the second and that businesspeople should seek to be of service rather than to make money. 'Service' is now the rallying cry of business. This is no new thing. Business was also going for 'service' in the early 1920s. In looking at the case of service versus profit, Follett eschewed the either/or reductionist view:

When people talk of substituting the service motive for the profit motive, I always want to ask: Why this wish to simplify motive when there is nothing more complex? Take any one of our actions today and examine it. There probably have been several motives for it . . . We work for profit, for service, for our own development, for the love of creating something . . . But whatever these motives are labelled – ethical or service motive, engineer's motive, craftsman's motive, the creative urge of the artist, the pecuniary gain motive – whatever, I say, these various motives, I do not think we should give any up, but try to get more rather than fewer.[6]

What Follett is saying here is that motives are mixed. To abstract them into just one is to do violence to reality. It is better to understand our motives in their full complexity, the better to satisfy them. In business, we do want to make a profit but we also derive satisfaction from providing the good product. We like to be appreciated. We prefer to work in amity with our colleagues. There is no need and no value to make the profit motive the overriding one to which all the others become subservient. To do so impoverishes us and also reduces overall performance. Neither was she starry-eyed about the exclusive devotion of the professions to the service motive: 'The professions have not given up the money motive. I do not care how often you see it stated that they have. Professional men are eager enough for large incomes.'[7] There are many today who would say that the money motive is taking over from that of service in the professions. Doctors threaten to go on strike; teachers go slow; academics seem to be more concerned with promoting themselves than in educating their students; the legal profession is under fire. One could go through the gamut of all the professions and find the service ideal dimmed indeed, and some times quite subsidiary to that of personal profit and personal advancement.

The Upkeep of Standards

One of the objects of the professional association is related to standards: to establish standards, maintain and improve them; to keep their members up to standards; to educate the public to appreciate standards and also protect it from transgressing members; but professional associations today are seen more as cosy closed shops intent on maintaining their privileges than as standard-bearers. In some cases, governments have had to intervene to break up a monopoly which was operating against the public interest.

So it is not sufficient merely to promulgate standards, but essential to ensure that they are maintained. Here, it is interesting to observe that whilst there has been a lowering of standards in the professions, standards in the business world have been going up. Seeking quality and excellence, developing high standards of business pride, business integrity and business honour – these are some of the ways of creating nice counterpoints to the professional standards and also giving the professions something to emulate. 'My word is my bond', the motto of the businessperson of honour, can stand comparison with any professional code. A business conscience can be as discriminating and as fine as any professional conscience and the businessperson, as often as the professional person, will forsake profit for principle. It is pleasing to note that women, now in increasing numbers in business, are turning out to be intrepid leaders in the field of business probity, integrating in happy balance moral and service and profit motives. These individual attitudes must play a part in shaping company policies and many companies are becoming very particular about the means used to make the profits. United Biscuits, for example, in its *Ethics and Operating Principles* booklet distributed to all its employees, puts it quite plainly:

Some employees might have the mistaken idea that we do not care how results are obtained, as long as we get results. This would be quite wrong: we do care how we get results. We expect compliance with our standard of integrity throughout the company, and we will support an employee who passes up an opportunity or advantage which can only be secured at the sacrifice of principle.

United Biscuits are not alone in setting their own standards of business conduct in specific detail and expecting 'everyone to live up to them'. This is becoming the norm amongst companies. The reason one does not hear much about them is because 'happy people have no history', the media invariably homing in on the transgressing individual or company.

The New Standards

Increasingly, new standards are emerging. The 'quality of earnings' of a company – whether they are well-balanced over activities and countries so as to make them reliable and stable over time – has always been carefully studied in the market in evaluating the company's performance and shaping its share price. Now, other criteria are coming to the fore. The activities which are being carried out by the company, its ways of doing business and the countries with which it is doing business are looked at critically to determine their acceptability or otherwise.

The most respected companies, the most admired ones, those that the liveliest young people want to work for are those who are ahead in their concern for social issues; those who are not waiting, for example, for government decrees to develop their environmental conscience but, of their own volition, are spending what is necessary to eliminate or reduce their own polluting, develop the ecological product or the more socially useful service. Their strong business conscience is attracting to them the ablest young people, and therefore the most likely to lead them to success.

In these companies, their wider vision encompasses much more than the aim of producing the short-term highest profit. Turning social problems into business opportunities; motivating and developing employees through better organization; innovating; investing for the long term; contributing to outside groups in the community – these are integral to their strategies and objectives and make for an exciting and enriching way of life for those working in them, and much the surer method of securing a regular and increasing profit.

As investors increasingly develop a social conscience and put their monies in those companies that satisfy their new aspirations, companies will find that an alpha plus rating in relation to the financial quality of its earnings will not attract sufficient investors if counterpoised by a gamma rating in relation to their social quality. Already, a company like The Body Shop which integrates its social concerns as a matter of course in its business policies has a rating in the City which is the envy of all.

Virtue is its own reward but, paradoxically, it brings, in addition, recognition and material profit. Capital is said to be blind and to go where it will produce the highest return. It is blind no longer. Investors more and more want it to go where it will have social value as well as produce a reasonable return. There need not be, and there is not, a dichotomy between the two.

The Place of Business in Society

Given the basic concepts in this chapter of the many faceted nature of the individual and of the business enterprise, it is not difficult to decide the proper place of business in society and the role that its directors and managers are capable of assuming in the wider society of which they are members. Follett found that their role went beyond the idea of being of service as expressing the altruism of human beings, praiseworthy as this may be. She found a deeper meaning to service: that of 'reciprocal service' and explained it in this way:

A group of people settling in a new region first plant and sow. But other things have to be done. One buys groceries and sells to his neighbours. He does this expecting someone else in the community to build his store and house and keep them in repair and someone else to make his shoes and someone else to look after him when he is ill and so on. This is an exchange, or interchange, of services. When we say 'reciprocal service', it seems to me that we are nearer the facts and also that we are expressing the give-and-take of life which is its noblest as it is its most profound aspect. That person is intellectually or morally defective who is not taking part in this give-and-take of life.[8]

She looked even more meticulously into that principle of reciprocation:

There is, however, a word which gives a truer idea of the place of business in society than even the expression 'reciprocal service' . . . the word 'function'. A businessman should think of his work as one of the necessary functions of society, aware that other people are also performing necessary functions; and that all together these make a sound, healthy, useful community. 'Function' is the best word because it implies not only that you are responsible for serving your community, but that you are partly responsible for their being any community to serve.[9]

Then, looking at the functions of the business, she was able to pinpoint perhaps its most important contribution to society:

I have left to the last what seems to me the chief function, the real service of business: to give an opportunity for individual development through the better organization of human relationships. Several times lately I have seen business defined as production, the production of useful articles. But every activity of man should add to the intangible values of life as well as to the tangible, should aim at other products than merely those that can be seen and handled. What does 'useful' mean, anyway? We could live without many of the articles manufactured. But the greatest usefulness of these articles consists in the fact that their manufacture makes possible those manifold, interweaving activities of men by which spiritual values are created. There is no overproduction there.[10]

And this was in fact what the forward-looking and wise business-people she knew were effectively doing in their companies:

It is the development of the individual involving the progress of society, that some of our finer presidents are aiming at, not pecuniary gain only; not service in the sense of supplying all our present crude wants, but the raising of men to finer wants . . . There are businessmen today who perceive that the *process* of production is as important for the welfare of society as the *product* of production.[11]

This is the crux of the matter. The way individuals are organized in their work relations to coordinate their contributions is as vital to the well-being of society as is the product or service which results therefrom.

Historically, process has been subsidiary to product and still is so in the main today. The aim is invariably to find 'the one best way' of connecting men and machines for highest productivity. Follett was amongst the few far-sighted ones who grasped the crucial importance to society of the organizing process itself. She saw it primarily as coordinating the energies of men, with its own unique function: enabling them to work more cooperatively together, it enables them, therefore, to evolve both in their personal development and in their solidarity with one another, in addition to enabling them to produce more and better. The good or service they produce meets the tangible needs and wants of society and improves its material welfare. The organizing process which unites them in cooperative effort in their daily lives makes them better individuals and, as such, makes for social progress. In the work-place, the production of tangible goods and of intangible values can combine to make the evolving community who, through tension and conflict but always with that underlying sense of consensus of the give-and-take of life, can move forward to new challenges and endeavours.

The work-place thus becomes an exemplar of the juster society, where the manager and the members of his team create new values and standards; and these new values and standards are radiated outwards, through the activities of the individual workers in the other groups to which they belong. Thus the better citizen at work becomes the better citizen in society. 'Our work' Follett said 'is to be our highest contribution to the community.'

Follett saw businesspeople and managers always as societal leaders, never as mere followers. She did not agree with those who held that 'management acknowledges as master the public will of the community alone'. She was quite adamant on that: 'The particular will of a particular community may have to be educated to appreciate certain standards.' It is for business management to provide that education and take the public forward. 'Business management' she told her audiences 'is responsible to something higher than the public will of a community' and 'its service to the public does not lie wholly in obeying the public.'[12] Business management has a higher responsibility: also to lead; not merely to provide what the public wants or to accept traditional wisdom.

Inventing the Future

To lead, it is necessary to invent the future. Just as businesspeople innovate in creating new products and services, they are also innovators in the field of organization, in the forms of organization they create to coordinate human relations at work. A recent interesting example of organization inventiveness is given by the National Freight Consortium which was floated to the public in 1989. The company, a pioneer in worker share ownership and wanting its employee-shareholders to retain control, gave them double voting rights and persuaded the financial markets and the investing public to accept what until then had been frowned upon and generally found unacceptable. A further exciting confirmation of the company's leadership is that the director who was the architect of many of the employee share-ownership breakthroughs, having completed this task at the National Freight Consortium, left to advise the Polish government on employee ownership.

As doers, directors and managers are not frightened to experiment and to learn from their experience, whether it be success or failure. This is why management, as Follett always held, is one of the most exciting activities in society: it offers the combined opportunity of meeting both its material as well as its moral well-being, the first through the provision of goods or services and the second through the more effective organization in the work-place.

The need for effective organization in the work-place has never been greater than it is today. The old hierarchical type of organization with its sequential command structure does not work and is generally discredited but still persists. The new technologies, the different demographics, the changed cultural milieu, the need for international cooperation regarding the environment – all this demands new forms of organization.

It is said that we are moving to the flatter organization; we talk a great deal about networks and about the networked organization but when one seeks to establish the organizing principle that will underpin the flatter or the networked organization, one is faced with the tattered remnants of the hierarchical syndrome. At a recent meeting extolling the inevitability and the virtues of the networked company, the speaker could only refer to the loosening of the hierarchical yoke, when asked about the organizing principle in the new structure. The implicit assumption is that organizations are inescapably hierarchical. We seem incapable of imagining a non-hierarchical work-place and automatically fall into the trap of hierarchical thinking.

What we need to evolve is a *relational* and not a *directional* view of the hierarchical principle. Traditional organization theory has always stressed that power, authority, influence and leadership are complex psychological concepts that can only be understood within the superior/subordinate framework. Follett explained them differently and came to different conclusions. Coordination and integration of information and action – very much as Follett was advocating over seventy years ago and now made easy by the technology which 'informates' – will undoubtedly take over from order giving as organizing principles.

Inventing the future is simpler if one looks back to make sure that one is not reinventing the wheel. I believe that the principles of partnership will come, more and more, to underpin working relations in the networked or flatter organization. These principles – of *uberrimae fidei*, of fullest disclosure of information, of trust, of being bound by each other's actions, of sharing in the profits and losses of the business, of pooling individual powers – regulate the relations of partners who see themselves as equals between themselves; not as absolutely or uniformly equal, but as each having something unique and different and worthwhile to contribute to the common endeavour and deriving their rights and responsibilities therefrom; an egalitarianism that includes the senior or managing partner; an egalitarianism that integrates different skills and different specialisms but is founded on a commonality of interests and of values.

It is these principles and values, most of them enunciated by Follett years ago, which are guiding the wisest managers of today and will increasingly guide the new managers of tomorrow in shaping the future of their businesses. The new managers will increasingly recognize and assume their total responsibility. At that hypothetical symposium of poets, politicians and priests, the best managers of today would already proudly proclaim that they are in business to be leaders; to lead their business and to lead society, always to be richer and fairer.

Notes

1 Mary Parker Follett, *The New State*, Longmans, Green, New York, 1920, p. 57.
2 Richard Dawkins, *The Selfish Gene*, Granada Publishing Ltd, 1982, p. 206.
3 Robert Axelrod, *The Evolution of Co-operation*, Penguin Books, 1990, p. 22.
4 John Spedan Lewis, *Fairer Shares*, Staples Press Ltd, 1954, p. 127.
5 Peter Drucker, *The Practice of Management*, Mercury Books, London, 1963, p. 343.
6 Mary Parker Follett, *Dynamic Administration: the Collected Papers of Mary Parker Follett*, Elliott M. Fox and L. Urwick, eds, Pitman Publishing, London, 1973, p. 116.
7 Follett, *Dynamic Administration*, p. 116.
8 Follett, *Dynamic Administration*, p. 104.
9 Follett, *Dynamic Administration*, pp. 104–5.
10 Follett, *Dynamic Administration*, pp. 111–12.
11 Follett, *Dynamic Administration*, p. 112.
12 Follett, *Dynamic Administration*, p. 109.

Appendix

Mary Parker Follett
(1868–1933): A Brief Biography

Sir Peter Parker, that practical manager in the highest reaches of business, in his recent autobiography, writes of Mary Parker Follett as 'one of the earliest of the bold standard-bearers in new management thinking'. He writes how 'just at the right moment of doubt, I found the right woman, Mary Parker Follett'; 'this prophetic woman' who 'had for me the most persuasive vision of them all'.

Mary Parker Follett has that unique quality: she inspires. All those who come into contact with her writings become her devoted followers. She inspires because she integrates the business organization and its management into the community and lights pathways for managers. Some would say that it is remarkable that a woman who was never herself a practising manager should have made such a timeless and enduring contribution to management thinking. I think the fact that she was a woman had something to do with it.

The Background

Mary Parker Follett was born in September 1868, in Quincy, near Boston, Massachusetts. Her father's precise occupation is unclear: one source says he was a mechanic, another a minor businessman and yet another a clergyman. There was a younger brother. There was money on the mother's side; her mother's father was a self-made man with 'fingers in most anything in Quincy that produced money'. It was this grandfather who would leave Follett well provided for. Her childhood was, however, far from happy. The mother was a chronic invalid and from very early on Mary had to run the household and had no time for play.

There was a close bond between father and daughter but he died when she was in her early teens. Already the domestic manager in the home, she now also had to take over the financial reins as well. Gradually, she assumed full business responsibility, 'attending in detail to their investments, inspecting personally the houses on which mortgages were held and carefully distinguishing between those which were flimsily built and those worth the risk of acquiring'. But there was no empathy between mother and daughter and Follett, in due course, was to sever all ties with her family.

At school, Follett was brilliant. She 'graduated' at the incredibly early age of 12 and went on to the Thayer Academy, one of the old-endowed schools, very important in the New England education system in the late 1800s. She spent some eight years there, coming under the influence of her history teacher, Miss Anne Thompson, a philosopher who had written a book on Fichte, and who did much to shape Follett's mind and teach her the methods of inductive reasoning. After leaving the Thayer Academy in 1888, Follett at 20 went on to study at the Society for the Collegiate Instruction of Women which had just been set up as an Annex to Harvard University, to allow women students who were not permitted to join Harvard to share in the benefits of a university education. Here, she came under the influence of Professor Bushnell-Hart, a very different kind of historian, a very down-to-earth historian, whose field was the study of the current American political scene. She became his intellectual protegee and it was from him that she acquired the art of unremitting attention to the detail of facts and the discipline of deductive reasoning. From the tutelage of these two, Miss Thompson and Professor Bushnell-Hart, she had forged a first-class analytical mind.

In 1890, at the age of 22, Follett came to England to study at Newnham College, Cambridge. She blossomed in the new, freer environment, made many friends and developed her lasting love for England. From the rather inexperienced girl who came to Cambridge, she returned to Boston a mature and assured young woman. She would recall with wonder, on her return to Boston, that one of her professors, Professor Sidgwick, had only two students, a Japanese student and herself; the Japanese man soon dropped out and the professor continued the full course for her alone. She found the stark contrast of this to her American academic experience remarkable.

When at Newnham College, she had read a paper on 'The Speaker of the House of Representatives' to the Historical Society which had been extremely well received. On her return to Massachusetts, she took time off from her studies to turn the essay into a book. Her professor, Bushnell-Hart, wrote in the foreword:

The book represents the strenuous labour of a well-equipped investigator for more than half of each year during four successive years. Whatever may be done by diligent search into the records, by visits to Washington, by conferences with ex-Speakers and by comparison of all the varied material, has been done by the author.

The book *The Speaker of the House of Representatives* appeared in 1896. A mixture of careful research and examination of the methods used by strong Speakers to exert their influence and power, the book astonished readers by its understanding of the subtle workings of the legislative process. Commentators were amazed that a woman outside Congress could understand and interpret its reality so perceptively and exactly. Theodore Roosevelt, reviewing the book for *The American Historical Review* (October 1896) declared it indispensable reading for any study of Congressional government. With this recommendation, it is no surprise that the book was a success and established Follett as an important writer in the political field.

Follett had taken time off from her studies to write the book. She returned to read economics, government, law and philosophy at the Annex, now renamed Radcliffe College and graduated from there in 1898 *summa cum laude*. She then went to Paris for post-graduate work and returned to Boston in 1900.

The Middle Years

When Follett returned to Boston, she was 32, unmarried and was to remain so. She had, years earlier, become friends with a Miss Isobel Briggs, an Englishwoman, some twenty years her senior. Gradually, this friendship developed 'into one of the closest, most fertile and noble friendships I have known' a mutual friend afterwards wrote, and continues:

For thirty years, they lived together. Isobel Briggs moved in the most distinguished circles in Boston and her friends accepted Mary as one of their intimates . . . Always there was the house in Otis Place to come to . . . There, Mary worked from very early on, all day, in fierce absorption . . . so utterly concentrated . . . that ordinary living and intercourse was for the time being suspended. Everything was burned up in a fierce white creative glow which left her exhausted, physically, nervously and mentally.

Miss Briggs was obviously wholly devoted to Follett. Another friend wrote that 'No one who did not share it will ever know what Isobel's contribution was: her entire subordination of herself to Mary's interests and work.'

Through Isobel Briggs, Follett became an accepted member of the then brilliant Boston and Harvard intelligentsia in that first Golden Age of Harvard. Follett's circle included the most forward-looking politicians, writers, philosophers, lawyers, businessmen as well as the Boston aristocracy of the time. She was to use her connections to the full. If she wanted to learn about a subject she was interested in, she would find, from amongst her friends, the authority on it, closet herself with him or her for the relevant time and come out, having got to the heart of it; and, if no immediate friend was an authority, there would always be someone who knew the foremost expert and was willing to put Follett in touch with that person.

Follett's Career

With a highly acclaimed study of the American political system behind her, an extensive academic education, and some years of close and valued involvement with the intellectual elite of Boston and Harvard, it was naturally assumed by her friends, when she returned to Boston from Paris in 1900, that she would follow her scholarly bent into academia. Instead she moved into social work. The remonstrations of her friends left her unmoved: she was going to do what she wanted to do, which was to involve herself in the activity of social work rather than follow the more passive career of the detached analyst.

In the Social Field

With her cast of mind, it was perhaps inevitable that she would become an innovator. Very quickly, she conceived the idea, unheard of then, of making full use of school buildings by getting them opened after school hours, for educational and recreational purposes. She said later that 'to provide special buildings, when the school buildings were already there, would have been bad management on our part'. With a collection of her friends, she opened the Roxbury Men's Club 'in a suburb of Boston which had so bad a name that policemen went into it in pairs'. Follett's determination was dauntless. On one occasion, some of the young men locked themselves in the bathroom with bottles of liquor and refused to come out. Follett was alone with Miss Briggs. She just told them she would get a ladder and come in through the window if necessary, whereupon they sheepishly filed out.

Initially, Follett had conceived the centres as community meeting places, not only for the young people flocking to Boston from the countryside with nothing to do in the evenings, but also for the local people to develop a direct responsibility for the social well-being of their neighbourhood. From community centres, they developed into school centres. In 1902, on a visit to London and Edinburgh, she had been impressed by the work on vocational guidance being done in the UK and, on her return to Massachusetts, she established placement bureaux in the school centres. She got Harvard and Radcliffe undergraduates to investigate the employment opportunities in the area, others to tabulate the abilities and skills of the young people who came to the centres and yet others to correlate the two and have the job matched to the person, already nicely packaged up, ready for the youngsters when they came in the evenings.

Follett partly financed from her own resources the early developments of the community and school centres. Her Boston centres became models for other cities to copy. In the next fifteen years, Follett got the school centres movement established and accepted, both practically and legally. They were finally incorporated into Boston's Public Schools System in 1917.

During those years in social work, Follett was the hands-on manager, initiating ideas, getting them accepted or adjusted, attending to the nitty gritty of detail and organizing the coordination of hundreds of disparate people to work in harmony, to achieve the plans they had developed together. When she found something which needed to be done, she would apply herself to a study of the subject and then make her eminently practical suggestions. Nothing was too insignificant for her to attend to; she would make, for example, a full study on the most economic way to bank the fires in the school centres before suggesting it to the janitors and convincing them to use it.

At the same time, ever the scholar, she was meticulously recording her experiences and learning from them. Follett was in fact learning at first hand the workings of the group-process: how people getting together influenced each other, developed their own plans and implemented them. She saw the creativity of the group-process and its potential value for self-government. She crystallized her new thinking in her next book: *The New State; Group Organization: the Solution of Popular Government* (1918).

This book was very different from her previous work in which she had investigated the rough-and-tumble of American politics and the exercise of power. In this new book, she was putting forward her own thinking about politics and government. Roughly, she was advocating the replacement of the bureaucratic institutions by group networks, where the local people themselves could combine together to think their problems and their needs through and work out their own solutions. It made a great impact, internationally as well as nationally. It earned the approbation of some of the foremost political thinkers in this country, including Lord Haldane. Quite out of the blue, he wrote to her in terms of high praise and asked to be allowed to write an introduction to the English edition – a great compliment indeed. Group networks are incidentally very much what we are moving towards, in our 'new' thinking.

Follett remained active in the social work field for 25 years and became an authority to whom local and national organizations would turn for advice and guidance. She always responded eagerly and constructively.

In the Public Field

These activities made her a public figure in Massachusetts affairs. She began to be inundated with requests to represent the public on arbitration boards, on minimum wage boards, on public tribunals and other similar official bodies. As a member of these committees, she became intimately involved in the politics of industrial relations. She saw how the two sides in any dispute would stay at arm's length, jockeying for position. She saw the strategems they employed to keep the upper hand, irrespective of the merits of the case. She realised that the parties to a dispute were not always directly and immediately concerned with finding a solution to their problems. This experience shifted her main interest from social work and political science to industry and business.

Much of the content of her next book *The Creative Experience* (1924) came from her experience in these new situations. This brought her a completely new and different audience: the businesspeople, many of whom asked for her help with their problems. Her advice, taken and acted upon so often, proved productive to the businesspeople and her reputation as a management advisor grew. She found the business world exciting, vital and alive. Unlike her other associates, the politicians, economists, academics and the like, the businesspeople were doers: if they liked an idea and thought it would work, they implemented it in their business to find out. This appealed to her scientifically trained mind.

In the Management Field

With her third book, a new chapter, a new area of endeavour now opened up for her. She was by no means a management consultant in the accepted sense of the term, but she would be asked to investigate specific problems in situ, or to study the big organizations and examine their structure to see if and how they could be improved. She would be asked to lecture at the annual conference of the Bureau of Personnel Administration in New York, prestigious events addressed by the foremost public figures in the country and attended by executives who came from all over the country. In England, Seebohm Rowntree, who was himself, in addition to being actively engaged in business, a pioneer in management thinking, would ask her to address the annual conferences he had started at Balliol College in Oxford. It was at Oxford that she met Lyndall Urwick who became a devoted follower. As her literary executor, he assembled and published in 1941 her lectures on management as a book, under the title of

Dynamic Administration: the Collected Papers of Mary Parker Follett, which book has been essential in propagating Follett's philosophy on management.

Follett's Last Years in London

In early 1926, Isobel Briggs died. The domestic anchorage Follett had relied on for 30 years had gone. She was devastated. Her good friends, the Cabots, brought her to Geneva later that year for a holiday. There, she met Dame Katharine Furse. Dame Katharine was very different from Follett. She came from an artistic and literary background. She had been a noted beauty and had married a painter. She was also a woman of action, a leader and a top administrator. During the First World War, she had become director of the Women's Royal Naval Service, with the equivalent rank of Rear Admiral. In 1917, she had been appointed Dame Grand Cross in the newly created Order of the British Empire. Later, she had taken up Girl Guide work and, in 1926, when they met, she was Director of the World Association of Girl Guides and Girl Scouts. Dame Katharine had by then been a widow for many years and, as her two sons were now grown up and in the Navy, she lived alone. She and Follett became friends. After a holiday together in Italy, they decided to set up house together, which they did in Cheyne Place, Chelsea, Follett taking over the top floor of the house.

In London, Follett renewed her old acquaintances and made new friends. In early 1933, when the Department of Business Administration (now the Department of Industrial Relations) was opened at the London School of Economics, she was asked to give the series of inaugural lectures, for which she adopted the theme of 'Freedom and Coordination'. These lectures are a distillation of her management philosophy. Lyndall Urwick again collected them and published them later under the same title. A short book, it encapsulates the essence of her teaching on management and is the quickest introduction to it.

Despite her increasing recognition and these further activities, the move to London seems not to have been a very happy one for Follett. Unbeknown to all, she was a sick woman. In late 1933, she had to go hurriedly to Boston to attend to her financial affairs. Whilst there, she went into hospital for a goitre operation. It was found that she was terminally ill with cancer. She died in hospital on 10 December 1933. A brave, pioneering life had ended. Her teaching lives on.

Index

Developmental Management

The following titles have now been published in this exciting and innovative series:

Ronnie Lessem: *Developmental Management* 0 631 16844 3
Charles Hampden-Turner: *Charting the Corporate Mind** 0 631 17735 3
Yoneji Masuda: *Managing in the Information Society* 0 631 17575 X
Ivan Alexander: *Foundations of Business* 0 631 17718 3
Henry Ford: *Ford on Management** 0 631 17061 8
Bernard Lievegoed: *Managing the Developing Organization* 0 631 17025 1
Jerry Rhodes: *Conceptual Toolmaking* 0 631 17489 3
Jagdish Parikh: *Managing Your Self* 0 631 17764 7
John Davis: *Greening Business* 0 631 17202 5
Ronnie Lessem: *Total Quality Learning* 0 631 16828 1
Pauline Graham: *Integrative Management* 0 631 17391 9
Alain Minc: *The Great European Illusion* 0 631 17695 0
Albert Koopman: *Transcultural Management* 0 631 17804 X
Elliott Jaques: *Executive Leadership* 1 55786 257 5
Koji Kobayashi: *The Rise of NEC* 1 55786 277 X

* Not available in the USA   All titles are £18.95 each

You can order through your local bookseller or, in case of difficulty, direct from the publisher using this order form. Please indicate the quantity of books you require in the boxes above and complete the details form below. NB. The publisher would be willing to negotiate a discount for orders of more than 20 copies of one title.

Payment

Please add £2.50 to payment to cover p&p.

☐ Please charge my Mastercard/Visa/American Express account
card number ☐☐☐☐☐☐☐☐☐☐☐☐☐☐☐

Expiry date _____
Signature _____
(credit card orders must be signed to be valid)

☐ I enclose a cheque for £_____ made payable to **Marston Book Services Ltd**
(PLEASE PRINT)

Name _____
Address _____

_____ Postcode _____

Tel No _____
Signature _____ Date _____

Please return the completed form with remittance to:
Department DM, Basil Blackwell Ltd
108 Cowley Road, Oxford OX4 1JF, UK
or telephone your credit card order on 0865 791155.

Goods will be despatched within 14 days of receipt of order. Data supplied may be used to inform you about other Basil Blackwell publications in relevant fields.
Registered in England No. 180277 Basil Blackwell Ltd.

DATE DUE

FEB 26 1998			

Demco, Inc. 38-293